DEAR TRINITY

Other Books by this Author

O Come, Let God Adore Us
And Other Sermons for Advent and Christmas

Not Exactly What They Expected
And Other Sermons for Holy Week and Easter

God's Purpose for Your Faith
And Other Sermons from Mark, Hebrews, James and 1ˢᵗ Peter

DEAR TRINITY

Letters from a Pastor to His People

Al Hill

SOMMERTON
HOUSE

ISBN: 978-1-948773-00-3 (sc)
ISBN: 978-1-948773-01-0 (hc)
ISBN: 978-1-948773-02-7 (e)

Library of Congress Control Number: 2018902495

Dedication

To the members of Trinity Christian Fellowship,
past and present—
who felt led to become a new church,
and then dedicated themselves
to living together
as a community of faith in Jesus Christ—
for calling me to lead them
in our remarkable spiritual adventure,
and for loving me
far beyond anything
my life or work with them
deserved.

Contents

Indices

Preface

In the spring of 2011, several hundred people in the Pinehurst, North Carolina, area decided to leave the historic interdenominational church they were attending and form a new congregation (also interdenominational). They named this new church "Trinity Christian Fellowship," meeting first in the Pinehurst Village Hall, then a hotel ballroom and, finally, a private high school's theatre. Before long, spaces were rented around town for administrative offices, classrooms and a fellowship hall, and ministries of all kinds emerged from the inspiration and imagination of the congregation. A search was begun for an appropriate parcel of land to be purchased as the site for a new and permanent facility.

Key members of the staff from the old church assumed similar positions with the new one, and the Senior and Associate Pastors from the other church, both men with long careers as Navy Chaplains behind them in addition to their years as pastors, were soon called as co-pastors. After a year, the elder of the two ministers decided to assume a reduced role in leadership (as Pastor Emeritus), and the church decided to promote the other, younger co-pastor (me) to the position of Senior Pastor. This transition marked the beginning of the letters in this volume.

෨෧

Being a vibrant, healthy church is a high standard to maintain when a congregation is well-established and its facilities are adequate to meet its needs (and already paid for). Giving birth to, and nurturing, a new fellowship without a long, common history and essential resources is "another thing again." Thank God we didn't have to do it without His help!

During our time together, Trinity went from one worship service to two, and then to three—from one Sunday School program to two. We were eventually prevented from building on the property we had purchased, so the beautiful building we had designed became a dream permanently deferred. Instead, God provided us an existing church facility in a better location, which we purchased and refurbished to meet our needs.

৯৵৶

When the church invited me to become their first Senior Pastor, I decided to add a weekly pastoral (or "PastorAl") letter to my ministry efforts as a way to communicate with the members of the fellowship about our progress in our shared life of faith—to help them appreciate that, despite the many things we seemed to lack, we were actually among the most vibrant and healthiest of churches.

Our Director of Family Ministries began editing and publishing a weekly email newsletter soon after we formed Trinity, to provide timely information about our ministries and activities. And a letter from me to "headline" the update seemed a natural fit (and a way to get more of our members to spend more time reading what we sent out each week).

And so, I wrote a letter a week for the better part of three and a half years, skipping a week or two between Christmas and New Year's—and several weeks during a vacation. When I wrote the letters, they were untitled. The titles have been added here so that you will have some sense of what each letter will be about without having to read it all the way through. In addition, most of the names of Trinity members in the letters have been removed.

Not all the letters I wrote are included in this collection. Most of the letters that "didn't make the cut" were devoted to practical matters of program promotion and volunteer recognition. When I didn't need to remind our people of what meeting was being held on Thursday or announce who had been elected to the Church Council, I tried to look for things in the normal routine of life that could comfort or inspire or intrigue our people in a spiritual way. Those are the letters you will find in the pages that follow.

కోుⁿ

After four years with Trinity, I decided it was time for me to retire from full-time pastoral ministry—a painful but correct decision. Letters 63 through 80 were written after I had announced that decision to the congregation.

I was pleased to be able to turn over my duties as Senior Pastor to my successor during a worship service we led together a little over eight months after I announced my plans. I left Trinity, loving the congregation, and being loved by them, as much as when my tenure with them had begun. That remains a source of great joy to me.

And now I hope that you will find something in these letters that will comfort or inspire or intrigue you in a spiritual way. If our Lord could take scraps of food prepared for others and feed multitudes, perhaps He will take these scraps of writing, prepared for the folks who made up the Trinity family, and use them to feed you as well.

కోుⁿ

Letters

1.

The First Letter

11 July

Several weeks ago, you voted to make me your Senior Pastor, and though I do not officially assume that position until the 1st of August, I thought I should start "moving in that direction" already. I wanted to start talking with you about our life together as a church and what we have to look forward to as God leads us where He wants us to go, together with Him.

And so, I plan to use this weekly update to share my thoughts and vision with you, knowing that there really isn't much opportunity to talk with you about these things when we gather together on Sunday or during the week. The first thing I want to share is my appreciation—for your affirmation of my ministry with you thus far, and for the honor you have shown me in calling me to this new position. I love you and I thank you and I will need even more of your prayer—and practical—support. And I am thankful that my God is able to supply all my needs, including the ones for being an effective senior pastor.

We are a miracle church. We have seen the hand of God at work among us in remarkable ways. I do not believe God is done doing miracles for us and with us, and I am thrilled that we will be experiencing God together.

૭ર્લ્ડ

2.

Feeding the Multitude

18 July

Monday and Tuesday of this week, we replicated one of the miracles of Jesus: we fed a multitude.

Every summer, our men's and women's ministries feed the local high school football players during their training camp—every last one of them. We don't start with five loaves and two fish the way Jesus did, but the food piles up—the loaves become hundreds of sandwiches.

But the miracle is not how much food there is, but how much these guys can eat. These big, young boys (did I mention they are big?) have an amazing hunger, and they aren't shy about feeding themselves on the food we provided. They don't wait for us to feed them. When they're told they can have the food, they "come and get it." And they don't wait long to come back for "seconds."

Trinity is a training camp for another team—God's team. Every one of us should have an amazing hunger for the food God brings for us. God provides a lot of spiritual food, in worship, Bible study and fellowship. God is not just being nice to us; He has brought us the nourishment for what the team exists to do: to go out and win.

Hungry people don't wait for somebody else to feed them—they "come and get it." And when they have consumed what God has provided, they don't sit around, reflecting indefinitely on how good the food was. They get back to training or gear up to play the game.

Trinity is a team. We have big appetites, so feed on His Word. Feed yourself through the Holy Spirit. And get in the game for which God is feeding your soul.

છે•જ

3.

An Afternoon in Heaven[1]

18 September

Everybody should have a chance to spend some time in heaven and see what it's like. That's what I did on Sunday afternoon. I spent a couple of hours in what seemed like heaven.

Heaven is like being the guest of honor at a great banquet in a beautiful room filled with people you love. And the people you've known the longest and love the most are the ones who are the closest to you. Everybody there is happy, and they seem to be happy for you because they love you and they're glad you're there.

In heaven, there is beautiful music, and from time to time, you all sing together songs you've known and loved and sung all your life. People you know and love stand up and tell everybody about special, inspiring moments you spent together when they blessed you, and make it sound as though it was the other way around, and make it sound as though all you ever do is wonderful things like that.

In heaven, the sun is shining and, no matter what's on the menu, your plate is filled with all the foods you love most.[2] And

---

[1] The Trinity congregation held a catered luncheon after church in a beautiful facility nearby to celebrate my becoming the church's first senior pastor.

[2] I was well-known for being a very "picky" eater, and so they had the chef prepare a special plate just for me.

after they've fed you and praised you, they give you incredible gifts you do not deserve just to show you how much they love you.

And then they ask God Himself to keep it coming—to keep on blessing you, and to sustain and even deepen the love they feel for you and you feel for them.

In heaven, nobody talks about the other stuff—the sins you've committed, the mistakes you've made, the dumb stuff you've done all your life. It's like those things don't exist. You only get the sense that no matter how glorious the present is, everybody knows the future you're going to spend together will be even better, and the knowledge of that thrills them all. And all the time, though nobody says it, you know everybody is thinking: "Surely the presence of the Lord is in this place."[3]

Everybody should have a chance to spend some time in heaven and see what it's like. Thank you for making my Sunday afternoon "heavenly."

੭৹৻

---

[3] "Surely the Presence of the Lord is in This Place," Lanny Wolfe, 1977.

4.

"Defining" versus "Describing"

25 September

In our Bible study this past Monday, I got rolling on a "spontaneous sermonette" about the difference between "defining" and 'describing" when it comes to sharing our faith. Most of us are not very good at "defining" really important spiritual things—like God or the gospel or our faith. For one thing, it's too hard to do subjects like that justice. It's like an old joke that used to go around my seminary in the form of a question on a fictitious final exam: "Define Creation and give two examples."

Our efforts to define God or the gospel for other people also invites debate and disagreement. Trying to come up with useful definitions is a fairly thankless and contentious job. So maybe we shouldn't bother.

৯৯৩

But "description" is another story. In fact, description is story. It's your story and my story and our story. When we describe what we have experienced in our relationship with God—when we describe what Christ has done for us and with us—when we describe what this fellowship has meant to us—we are sharing our faith, the gospel, and God.

You can dispute a "definition." Not so, a "description." It's what you experienced—what you saw and heard and felt. Who can argue with that? And the beauty of description is that *you* can describe as easily as I or any pastor what God has done in your life—what you have experienced in Trinity.

Let me encourage you: Don't let yourself feel defeated by the difficulty of "definition." Instead, delight yourself in the freedom and power of "description."

❧

5.

After the Election

Writing the day after the elections, I know that most of us are reacting to the results. Half the country is elated, and half is deeply disappointed. Half of America is filled with hope for the future and half of the country despairs about what lies ahead. You and I are not unaffected by these great political events; we are blessed to be citizens who are able to participate in the political process and we have been taught to believe that we have a right to help form the government that governs us.

But we Christians are also citizens of another government: the kingdom of God. We have sworn allegiance to a Leader whose authority is not derived from the democratic will of the people but from the sovereign will of a gracious God.

The hope of an election is that your candidates will be chosen. The fear of an election is that they will not. There is no such concern in the kingdom of God because the only election in this realm is God choosing you. And His term of office as your Leader is not two years, or four, or six—but all of life and all of eternity.

Now that the earthly election is over, the candidates—winners and losers alike—will take some time to go away and rest. The demands upon them have been heavy and they need to be renewed.

Jesus called the first citizens of His kingdom, on occasion, to come away from the normal demands of life and ministry to spend time alone with Him. It is a good idea for us to do the same.

৵৵

6.

Be Thankful for the Future

21 November

Since tomorrow is Thanksgiving, it seems only right to make that the subject of my letter to you this week. Last Wednesday, we took time after our family-style, covered dish dinner to hear what everybody was thankful for. It was a simple, but moving, experience. As always, we have much to be thankful for, and seeing those you love, and having more food than you can eat, can certainly put you in a grateful frame of mind.

For me, every Thanksgiving now is experienced against the backdrop of the memories of the Thanksgivings of my childhood. I remember going to my grandmother's house and seeing almost as many relatives as we had people in Trinity Hall,[4] all eating and talking and playing together. We tend to look to the past and the present to find the things for which we are thankful.

---

[4] Shortly after forming Trinity, we leased office space on the south side of town. We also needed a larger space for Wednesday night dinners and other weekday activities. The local Catholic Church graciously invited us to meet in their fellowship hall our first summer, which gave us time to find and rent an old house near our offices that had previously served as the local American Legion Hall. We promptly re-christened it "Trinity Hall," and made extensive and wonderful use of it until we moved into the church facility we purchased three years later.

But this morning, I got to thinking about being grateful for what lies ahead—for what God is going to do for us—and give us—in the future. Because our God is a gracious and merciful God—and because He is *"the same yesterday and today and forever"* (Hebrews 13:8)—we may have confidence that God will be just as generous in the days and years and eternity to come as He has been thus far. And so I started "counting blessings" that haven't come yet, but will.

I am thankful for what God is going to do with Trinity in the next year. I'm grateful for the help God is going to give individuals who will encounter hardship, and for the comfort He will give to those who will lose loved ones. I'm grateful that those of us who will finish this earthly journey next year will have a place in heaven to go to where our eternal reward is waiting. I'm grateful that those of us who will still be here at the end of the year will enjoy another wonderful and miraculous year together.

You get the point: as you consider the scope of your gratitude, do not shortchange yourself. God is good—past, present and future. The Psalms say over and over:

> *"O give thanks unto the Lord*
> *for He is good.*
> *His steadfast love endures forever."*

The best is yet to come.

❧

7.

"Wanting" versus "Expecting"

28 November

I've been working on the Wednesday evening lessons on the background and message of Christmas carols. I decided to start with a couple of hymns that are, more accurately, Advent carols. "Come, Thou Long-Expected Jesus!" is the title and first line of one of them, written in 1744 by Charles Wesley.

The word "advent" means "arrival" or "coming into being." If you capitalize it, it refers to the coming of Christ into the world. We use it mostly to mean the four weeks or so before Christmas the Church has set aside for us to reflect on how much our world needs a Savior, and to prepare ourselves to celebrate the birth of Jesus, and to remind ourselves of His promised return. The Church season of Advent begins this Sunday.

Without giving all my lesson away, I wanted to point out something that just occurred to me. We usually think of the people of the Old Testament wanting God's Messiah to come and save them. As Christians, we rejoice that He finally did. But Wesley picks up on something else. They didn't just want Jesus to come— they expected Him to—for centuries. Even if they did not know what His Name would be when He arrived, they expected Jesus to come.

It's commonplace to ask children (even the older ones like us), "What do you want for Christmas?" But it might make for an interesting and instructive, and perhaps even inspirational, exercise to ask, "What do I *expect* from God as I enter this Advent season—the time of celebrating the arrival of Jesus and awaiting His Return? Do I *expect* what God has promised?"

Wesley calls Jesus the "dear Desire of every nation," as well as "long-expected." But desire and expectation are very different things. Expectation implies a level of confidence that something is going to happen—a certainty of result, even if the timetable is unclear. The reason God makes promises and keeps them is so that we may have expectations and not merely desires—that we may live our lives expectantly and not just wishfully.

What you expect of God will affect what God may, in turn, expect of you. I just mention that because this Sunday, the first Sunday in Advent, is our Celebration Sunday when we tell God what He may expect from us in the year before us.

I expect our Lord will come to us with power and wonder and blessing as we look for His Return.

And what may God expect of you?

෧ー෬

8.

Our First Family Album

11 December

This is an exciting day. Today (or rather tonight) we begin distributing the new pictorial directory of our Trinity family. We have been working long and hard to get it to you, so you can get to know each other better.

The pictorial directory—and the name tags we all wear every Sunday morning—are both tools to help us build our fellowship. When we started, we did not "have" a church—we had no facility of our own to come to to worship. But we understood from the first that we were a church. We were "one in the bond of love."[5] I know and love you all, but you do not all know each other, and so you are not able to love each other as you can and should. With the directory, you will be able to put a lot more names to faces.

But more than that, you will be able to build more relationships—Christian relationships—with your Trinity brothers and sisters. It is not enough to know a name. God would have you take the next step and approach people you have hesitated to approach because you didn't know their names. As you go through the pictures, pick some people out that you haven't spoken to before and speak to them. You could start the conversation with something like, "I saw your picture in the directory and just wanted

---

[5] From "The Bond of Love," Otis Skillings, 1971.

16

to say, 'Hello.'" The people you normally visit with during the fellowship time won't mind if you expand your interaction, especially if they're doing the same thing. We are a wonderful group of people. I would love for you to get to know everybody the way I do.

Of course, you will see people on Sunday or Wednesday night, or at one of our special events, that you don't recognize—whose pictures aren't in the directory. Some will be members, but some will be guests—your guests, because you are Trinity, and anyone visiting Trinity is visiting you.

Did you know that we have added you to the Trinity Welcoming Committee? We assign "Greeters" to the doors on Sunday to shake hands and say "Hello!" and "Welcome!" You could even turn the directory greeting around and say, "I didn't see your picture in our new directory, but just wanted to say, "Hello."

Starting tomorrow, our pictorial directory will start becoming obsolete. I hope it will do so rapidly—because so many new people are joining us who will have to have their pictures taken to be added to the ones already there. Our photographers can add more pictures, but you will have to add more people to our family by welcoming them *to* it, and then, *into* it.

Get the picture?

৯৹৽৻

9.

Christmas People[6]

This will be the last weekly update sent out before Christmas, and I could not miss this opportunity to wish you all the joy that is ours as disciples of our Lord Jesus Christ, the Christmas Child. We are like the shepherds who heard the angels and beheld this gracious, glorious Gift of God. We were told what God was doing and we came to the place where Jesus was and found that what we had been told—that He was our Savior—was true. And from that time on, we have experienced life differently—and people around see the difference.

But even more than the shepherds, we are like Mary and Joseph, who made Jesus their own when they really didn't know what that meant—and lived with Him and loved Him and experienced His love for them every day. Every day, we are the family of Jesus. Every day, we live our lives with Him, remembering, amid whatever is happening, what happened when He came into our lives that first special day.

We are Christmas people. Wherever we are, we will go in our spirits to Bethlehem, to await and worship the Holy Child. And we

---

[6] Yes, a good portion of this pastoral letter found its way into the preface of *O Come, Let God Adore Us!*, the collection of Advent and Christmas sermons I published several years ago.

will not leave Christmas without Him, because He has been born to us. For you and me and all of us, Christmas will never end. Enjoy the lights, knowing the Light of the world will remain. Enjoy the gifts you give and get, knowing that the greatest Gift of all is already yours. Enjoy the love of family and friends, knowing that Love divine, all loves excelling,[7] has filled your heart for all eternity.

Christ the Savior is born! Wrap Him in your love and lay Him in your heart.

అ•◌

---

[7] See "Love Divine, All Loves Excelling," Charles Wesley, 1747.

10.

The "Annex"

I am a retired Navy Chaplain. Though I am very focused on Trinity Christian Fellowship and my ministry with you, once in a while, something from my Navy past pops up to remind me of my many years in uniform. That's what happened today.

A retired Chaplain friend of mine sent me an article about the eminent demolition of the Navy Annex in Washington. The "Annex" is a sprawling eight-wing, four-story eyesore built at the beginning of World War II to be a temporary government warehouse. When completed, it was, instead, turned into offices for the Navy and Marine Corps. It has been the home of the Navy Chief of Chaplains ever since.

I worked there when I was on the Chief of Chaplain's staff. Now, the government is going to tear down this 70-year old building.

It is hard to imagine the Annex not being there on the hill overlooking the Pentagon. It is a sad thing to see a significant part of your past slipping away. But it is an exciting thing to sense a significant part of the future slipping into place. When the "temporary" Annex is gone, the ground will become part of an expanded Arlington National Cemetery, the permanent resting place for our nation's heroes.

The present is always slipping into the past. But the future is always on the verge of becoming the present. Our future as a family of faith is coming to meet us, and what makes our future different from our present and our past is that our future will bring with it a transition from the temporary to the permanent.

Like the Annex, our past and our present have been experienced in temporary facilities. We began with nothing and scurried to find places to worship and study together, to share fellowship and to conduct our administrative business. And God always provided for our needs—He blessed us time and time again with wonderful facilities. But they have, and remain, temporary.

Eventually, what is temporary goes away; only what is permanent endures. It is fascinating, though, how easily the temporary can take on the appearance and feel of permanence—and how difficult it can be to transition into the permanent and out of the temporary.

In significant ways, our future as a fellowship will begin this year. We will live with the temporary for a while longer. But we are moving in the direction of the permanent, for that is what our future holds. Our future is coming, and so is our permanent home. And both belong to God.

☙◦❧

11.

The Healing Service

6 February

Later today, a small group of us will meet, as the sun is setting, in the Ministry Center.[8] We will come to take part in our monthly Healing Service. This quiet gathering of souls comes a week earlier than usual this month because Ash Wednesday falls on the second Wednesday, the day we usually meet.

But even though it will be a week early, the experience will be the same: soft lights in the back of the room will join with the flickering flame of candles on a table set for Communion, all centered under a cross to suggest the sacredness of the occasion. Around the table, a double row of black, folding chairs convey the simple and humble nature of the event. In the far corner, a massive cross[9] stands as a reminder of the One Who suffered upon just such a cross for our sins—and, in that way, shared in our suffering, taking it upon Himself. And before the cross there is a kneeling

---

[8] The Ministry Center was part of the complex of spaces we leased in a small shopping center just outside of town for weekday activities and offices. The Ministry Center had been a store of some kind, but became a multi-purpose meeting room (after some renovation, a hard cleaning, and several coats of paint), with a separate room for child-care. Our administrative offices were next door.

[9] The cross was beautifully crafted by one of our members. It sat in an ornate base and was about six feet high—and, being solid wood, was very heavy.

bench, inviting each to "come to the Cross" in prayer, and in prayer, to leave our burdens with the Lord of the Cross. It is a beautiful service—a powerful service—an intensely spiritual service. And there is healing: sometimes for the body; always for the soul.

But, of course, there are unofficial healing services going on all the time at Trinity. As a congregation, we have been remarkably healthy physically. But still, there are many of you who suffer every day. Some of the suffering is known and shared within our fellowship and thus the subject of many and constant prayers.

Some of you bear burdens of pain or sorrow privately, sharing only with God in the secret places of your hearts. Even in our short time together, beloved brothers and sisters have been taken from us by their illnesses, to be healed—finally and forever—of all sickness and suffering, by the Great Physician Himself.

And for those of us who tarry awhile in this earthly realm of diseases and injuries, disappointments and loss, the mystery is not so much that suffering is our lot—it is part and parcel of this life for everyone—but that there is hope of healing, and enough healing—miraculous healing—to encourage and sustain our hope as believers. The mystery for us Christians is that God has provided us so much joy despite our suffering—in the midst of our suffering—that our suffering is transformed into the source of much of our spiritual power. Someone has said, "We become most like our Savior in the sharing of His suffering" (Philippians 3:10).

We pray for healing—rightly—but we do so always in the confidence that we are praying to the One Who ever holds us in the center of His love.

☙❧

12.

Getting Well

I've been thinking about the business of "getting well." I don't know if you've noticed, but it has occurred to me recently that a number of our folks who have suffered accidents or struggled with illnesses or undergone replacement or corrective surgeries have been recovering—getting better—getting stronger. I wish it were true for all of you who have been sick or injured.

Some of you know pain every day and have to summon great courage to even attempt the simplest tasks. We know of some of the burdens you bear, and gladly pray for you. Other things, no one knows. And we would be very humbled if we did know about the difficulties some of you endure in secret.

The trajectory of life for all of us leads ultimately and inevitably to the weakening of our bodies and even our minds. And so we celebrate and thank God when we can point to an injury mending or an illness subsiding. All healing is really miraculous.

❧

Our being a Christian fellowship is also about our "getting well." Our spirits suffer their own injuries and illnesses as we go through this life. We suffer at the hands of others, and from circumstances no one intended. And we inflict many wounds upon ourselves.

The hurts we experience are sometimes suffered in silence. Other times, our emotional and spiritual maladies are contagious: we pass on to those close to us something of what bothers us.

But Trinity is a place where people get well spiritually, because there is a Great Physician among us Who loves us and knows how to mend the broken heart and bind up the wounded spirit. Our Lord gives us the divine medicines to cure the soul and the holy confidence to believe that we can get stronger spiritually every day we live—even when our bodies discover new difficulties and our minds will not serve us with the clarity and confidence they once did.

Many of you have shown me that the spirit does not have to diminish with the ravages of age. The hardships of mind and body will often strengthen the soul if you can bring the right therapy to bear—if you can tap into the great supply of grace God makes available to us as we meet one another's needs and help bear one another's burdens when we are able to do so. With each other's help, we are "getting well" spiritually—getting better—getting stronger—all the time.

We sense that the people we are becoming is a miracle, too. Even as we seek to overcome our own hurts, we look for opportunities to offer compassion and caring treatment to each other. In that way, we become, with His help, like our loving Savior: "wounded healers" (1 Peter 2:24), reaching out to help others as He reaches in to us to restore our souls.

ॐ∞ड़

13.

Just Stop and Think

6 March

Do you ever just stop and think about something for a few minutes? I think people used to do more of that than they do now. There's too much on our "agendas" these days; we have to keep moving—and keep our minds moving—from one thing to the next, just to keep up. There's also too much "interference"—too much going on around us all the time, competing for our attention.

Sometime today, see if you can stop what you're doing— whatever you're paying attention to or whatever is keeping you from paying attention at all—and think about this: Today you are a Christian. Just think about that for a few minutes.

And as you do, be careful not to fall into the self-inflicted guilt-trip mode of thinking. Don't start asking yourself, "What kind of Christian am I?"

Just think about the simple fact: You are a Christian. Today— now—that's what you are. That is the reality of your life. You are a person who is in a real, interactive, redemptive, blessed relationship with Jesus Christ. You are connected to Jesus—right now—with all that Jesus brings to that relationship.

So many people are not Christians—have not asked for or experienced what you have received from Jesus. But you have asked. And you have received. And so, you are a Christian.

If you think about that for a few minutes—if you let your mind turn it over and around—you'll have other thoughts about being a Christian that wouldn't come to mind unless you gave your mind a little time to ponder the implications and applications.

I took a few minutes to think about that simple fact and it occurred to me that whatever I experience today, the fact of my being a Christian won't change. Everything that happens to me today will happen while I am a Christian, and my being a Christian will give everything that happens its meaning.

It also occurred to me as I thought about being a Christian today that just as I'm thinking about Jesus, Jesus is thinking about me. Just as I am happy to be a Christian, Jesus is happy that I am a Christian. Just as I want His help to get through this day, Jesus wants to help me get through this day.

I thought a little longer and I thought of something else: just as I am a Christian today, when I wake up tomorrow, I will still be a Christian. It occurred to me that this is true whether I wake up in this world or in eternity—all because I am a Christian today.

I suppose if I stopped and thought a few minutes more about this, I would think of some more things, but I probably shouldn't press my luck. It's probably best to start small and work your way up when it comes to "stopping and thinking."

It's amazing what a few minutes of thinking about things like your faith can do for you, especially when Jesus is thinking about it with you.

What do you think?

৵৽৶

14.

Hearing One Another

10 April

You know that we are an interdenominational church. That alone makes us pretty unusual (in an accepting-of-differences sort of way). I've been thinking recently that we are also a "bi-lingual" church. No, I don't mean what you probably think I mean.

I know many of you can speak languages other than English. That's not what I'm talking about. But let me give you a hint: some years ago, a fellow named Gary Chapman wrote a book to help husbands and wives communicate better, or, at least, understand and appreciate better each other's attempts to communicate. The book is called *The Five Love Languages.*[10] Chapman's point was that different people express their love in different ways, and even if it doesn't sound like "love" to you, that's what the other person is saying—in his or her "language."

Chapman suggested that for couples to have healthier, happier marriages, each of the partners should try to become "bi-lingual." You know *your* "love language"—the way you express your love— and what says "love" to you. But you also need to learn some of that other person's "love language" so that you will understand

---

[10] Gary Chapman, *The Five Love Languages: How to Express Heartfelt Commitment to Your Mate*, Northfield Publishing, 1995.

28

when "love" is being spoken to you, and so that you can convey love effectively to someone else when that is what you want to say.

So what do I mean when I say we're a "bi-lingual" church?

It seems to me that across the spectrum of our fellowship, we speak two different "languages," to a greater or lesser degree. One is what I will call "the language of spirituality." It's "God-talk." It focuses on or expresses things in terms of the supernatural. Its vocabulary includes words and phrases like "miracle," "sense of the holy," "divine vision" and "eternal truth." A lot of us speak "the language of spirituality" fluently, and so we speak it frequently and enthusiastically.

But not all of us. Some of us speak another language: "the language of practicality." It is a language of more detail and specificity. It is a language more geared to describing present realities in quantifiable terms. It measures—tabulates—observes and evaluates earthly causes and effects—even in churches. It doesn't sound like "God-talk," and so it may not be heard as much in a church as the other language. But there are a number of our members who speak this language just as fluently as others speak "the language of spirituality."

And here's an interesting thing, and my point for bringing it up: both "the language of spirituality" and "the language of practicality" are authentic "faith languages." Both are ways of expressing deep, committed, genuine faith in God.

Sometimes we're tempted to forget that when we find ourselves listening to the language that is not our own "natural" tongue. But it's true. And I've discovered that all of us are really bi-lingual. Even those who speak "the language of spirituality" are not unaware of, or unconcerned about, practical matters related to the church. And those whose native tongue is "the language of practicality" are not unaware of, or unaffected by, the presence and moving of the Holy Spirit in their lives and our fellowship.

You may not be inclined to speak one or the other, but for a happier, healthier fellowship, it is important that we devote ourselves to learning and understanding and valuing both, because I suspect that the God Who is able to confuse languages, and to cause everyone to hear the gospel in his own language, speaks to us in both—both "faith languages."

৯৯

15.

Old and New

I had a birthday earlier this month. My age used to have the number "9" in it. Now it has a "0." For my birthday, my daughter, who has nothing higher than a "3" in her age, took me to "the phone store" to (as she put it to the even younger young lady behind the counter) trade in my "dumb" phone for a "smart" one. I never thought of my phone as dumb, but I did discover that I was after I had been in the store for a few minutes. I suppose I should have been grateful that *I* wasn't being traded in.

I took my daughter with me because I knew I would need some moral support to survive the public demonstration of my technical incompetence that I anticipated. And I anticipated right.

It turned out I also needed a translator. The young lady never stopped talking, except for the split seconds from time to time when my daughter would confidently inject some essential bit of information (encoded, I think) in answer to a question I did not realize had been asked. Then they would both look over at me, which was my cue to nod at the animated but unintelligible clerk like one of those silent, cryptic bidders at some high-class art auction.

Then my daughter, who once talked to me in gibberish as a baby, resumed her conversation with this female font of undecipherable phone knowledge, speaking fluent gibberish again as a mature, well-educated adult.

The end result is that I am now the proud owner of what is (this month) the cutting edge of telephone technology. It's a slender slice of black metal and glass about the size and shape of a Hershey Bar (without almonds) that does not melt in my hand but allows me—without even knowing it—to call people I didn't mean to call, just by shifting my position in my chair. Fortunately, my concentration is not broken by people's voices in my pocket, repeating with increasing intensity: "Hello, *hello*, HELLO!" I simply don't hear them.

I'm told these new phones can hold the equivalent in information of 30,000 copies of the novel *War and Peace*. I'm also told that my phone can tell wherever I am in the world—to somebody—and a lot more about me and what I'm doing and thinking besides. I suppose that's a little scary, because who knows what that "somebody" is going to do with all that knowledge about me. The reason it's scary is that that "somebody" is not God.

God doesn't need me to have a new smart phone. God has always known exactly where I am, even when I have been hopelessly lost—physically and spiritually. God has always known what I was doing and thinking. God hears me even when I don't have enough sense to call on Him, and He speaks every language there is—including the one I speak and understand. The information He can hold onto far exceeds what my phone can remember; His knowledge and memory are infinite. He has numbered every hair on my head and supplies the air for every breath I breathe.

Next month or next year, my new phone will be old technology, just as I am becoming (increasingly) old technology, humanly speaking. My "dumb phone" will be discarded; its useful life over. But God will never discard me; I will be "upgraded" to eternity.

God is the ultimate technical expert for everything that exists, including you and me. And He loves us, which is not true of whoever it is who's tracking all the information about us these new phones are supplying. This causes me to think that the one word the phone clerk used that I did understand—she spoke it every time I nodded, in fact—might better be applied to God: "Awesome!"

৵৵

16.

On Stage

8 May

For two Sundays last month, our makeshift sanctuary at O'Neal[11] was even more makeshift than usual. Our altar and cross and "story rug"[12] and piano and choir—and the glorious image of our Risen Lord[13]—all of which normally drew us into worship, were crowded off the stage that was filled in their place with the make-believe props of a make-believe world—the set for the school's spring play.

A heavy black curtain was drawn across the front of the stage, cutting off the bright lights behind it we were accustomed to seeing (and seeing by)—blocking our view of what always inspired us.

---

[11] Several weeks after Trinity was formed, we were able to lease the Hannah Bradshaw Activities Center on the campus of The O'Neal School, a private school several miles northeast of the Village of Pinehurst proper, for our Sunday morning programs. We held our worship services in the theatre, gathered for refreshments and fellowship in the expansive foyer, and set up our nursery and Sunday School in several classrooms located in the building. When we referred to the facility, we called it simply, "O'Neal."

[12] This is what the youngsters called the beautiful oriental carpet we spread out each Sunday on the theatre stage floor for them to sit on to listen to the Children's Sermon.

[13] A 12-foot square movie screen could be lowered from the overhead in front of the back curtain of the stage, and to make the space seem more "church-like," we projected the dramatic image of a stained-glass window of the Ascension of Christ on it each Sunday.

And so, pushed to the edge of the stage and into deep shadows, we raised our cross higher and continued to proclaim the gospel in the darkness. We sang God's praise as best we could with what room we had left and what resources we could muster.

And then last week, the curtain was reopened, and the darkness was dispelled, and there was the Christ of the Resurrection as always, high and lifted up, even as Isaiah saw the Lord in the great Jerusalem Temple of his day (Isaiah 6:1). And we proclaimed the message of our Lord from the inspired Word of God in the light, just as we had in the darkness. It sure was good to be back in the light and on stage again with the things of the worship of our God.

What I have described to you—what you yourself experienced—is a parable of our experience in the world today. The world stage, once filled with the signs and symbols and sounds of the worship of Jesus Christ, has now been cluttered instead with all the props of the artificial, modern and increasingly godless world. The cast and crew putting on the world's presentation of make-believe have crowded out the things of God in order to show the world a performance of fiction. And a curtain of darkness is being drawn across the world stage so that the uplifting image of Christ and the light He brought to our world will be hidden from human view.

Faithful Christians are being pushed to the edges of the stage and forced to function under ever more challenging conditions. The curtain is closing now and will close further in the days to come. How long we will carry on in the shadows and on the edges of the world stage we do not know.

But carry on we will, because we know certain, vital truths. Behind the curtain of darkness, the light shines still. The darkness has not put out the light—it cannot! It has only obscured for a time the light that comes from a divine Source. The props of a make-believe reality that now fill the world stage are temporary and will eventually be destroyed, to be replaced one day by the eternal things of God.

And, as we discovered to our joy last Sunday, when the black curtain of evil is eventually drawn away from our world, our Lord will be there as He always was, in glorious light, to welcome us and inspire us.

Yes, we will be meeting our Lord in a make-shift sanctuary for some time to come. But our permanent place is coming—where the light will never go dark and the stage will never be crowded with other things, and we will see Him as He is. That is the eternal reality. And what we are going through in this world is like a play to show us, and prepare us for, the great script of glory God has written for us.

So, on with the show—God's show!

ॐ◦ॐ

17.

A Little Exercise

15 May

Here's a little exercise for you to try in the morning. (No, not the physical kind to get you all worn out before you even get started; but sort of a mental kind, to get your spiritual radar rotating before you launch out into your day.)

As you sit up on the side of your bed or step into the shower or start sipping your coffee, and whatever problem, burden, worry and frustration you have comes to mind (as they do every morning for most of us), ask yourself this question: "What might God do about this today?" And then let go of the leash you always keep your imagination tethered to.

Now, this is different from your morning prayers, where you ask God to do what you want Him to do, or what you think He should do. I'm just suggesting that you speculate a little bit. And don't quit with the first thing that comes into your mind.

What might God do about whatever you wake up to? God can do anything. God never runs out of good ideas (the way we do) for dealing with a problem that just won't seem to go away. God is never unwilling to try something (the way we are) because it looks too hard or too costly or too uncomfortable. The only reason God wouldn't try something is that it's the wrong thing to try, which, of course, He knows, being God and all.

So what could He do?

Technically, we know the list of possibilities is endless. But the question is actually a little different: "What might God do?" It assumes that God not only could do something—but that God may do something about what you're coping with—or not coping with, at least as well as you would like.

And if you start thinking about what God might do and you come up with a few ideas yourself, you might begin to think of that bothersome thing as something you're not dealing with alone. You might just start to realize that God is involved with you in that thing—because He's involved with you in everything. And now the whole thing takes on a whole different complexion.

And if you've spent a few minutes at the beginning of your day imagining what God might do, it's only natural to spend the rest of the day looking to see if you guessed right—about what God might do.

And it only stands to reason that you're much more likely to see something you're looking for than something you're not— which brings us to another mental exercise I want to suggest for the end of the day, as you crawl into bed and wait for sleep to come.

Ask yourself this question: "What did God do about that thing today?"

If you're still around to ask the question, that alone implies an answer to the question. And if you spent the day looking for what God might do, it stands to reason that you saw more of God than you would have if you hadn't started the day imagining, and then spent the rest of the day watching. This is true even if what you saw wasn't on the list of what you thought of in the morning.

And here's the cool thing about these little "games." By asking the question in the morning, you get more answers at night. And the more answers you come up with at the end of one day, the more possibilities you'll think of the next morning. And the more of God you'll see throughout the day.

Remember: "What might God do?" and "What did I see Him do?"

அ⊶ఞ

18.

Happy Birthday

One of the things we try to do at Trinity is to recognize and celebrate the special days of our members—birthdays and anniversaries. We show your pictures and dates on the screen as part of the program on Wednesday nights, and sing "Happy Birthday" to anybody there whose birthday falls in the following week. (Singing "Happy Anniversary to you!" doesn't really work musically, so we just clap for that.)

Two boxes of cards and envelopes appear on my desk at the beginning of every month (one for anniversaries and one for birthdays) so that I can write you (which I do—as with everything else—at the last minute). But I do not hurry through the process, because I have discovered that writing birthday and anniversary wishes each day gives me an opportunity to focus my thoughts on you individually rather than on "all of you"—on the fellowship as a whole.

"Don't you do that when you pray for me?" Yes, but when I pray for you personally, I am concerned about what you need God to give you or do for you. I am talking to God about your pain or sorrow, your struggles and crises.

When I write you to wish you "Happy Birthday," it is my opportunity to appreciate you—to think about who you are and how you bless our fellowship—and me. It doesn't take me long to figure out what I appreciate about you—what you do or how your personality makes Trinity a better, stronger church. There is not a person in our fellowship who does not contribute in a positive way to the life of our church. There is not a person here that I do not appreciate in some specific and particular way. And I look forward to telling you that on your special day.

৵•৶

19.

Power

How long were you without power? Not an uncommon question after last week's storm blew a few trees across a few electrical lines somewhere and the lights went out—and the TV went blank—and the telephones and internet went dead—and the air conditioner stopped cooling—ditto the refrigerator. I heard the question a few times before church Sunday. I asked it myself a few times.

And as soon as you answered the "How long…?" question (which we all could, because we all calculated it, so we could compare our suffering with each other), you probably broke into a description of what it was like for you—to be without power.

"I was just getting ready to…."

"I was right in the middle of…"

"I had been planning to…but forget that!"

"I couldn't do anything!"

For us, the power went out about 6:00 p.m., which wasn't so bad at first, because there was still some light outside, but not as much as there should have been, because the storm clouds blocked the sun. Later, as the darkness relentlessly settled in around us, we went hunting for that flashlight we keep somewhere, and candles (really just nubs left over from long ago and shoved in the back of drawers here and there). But when there's no power, you use whatever you can find that gives light, and you're thankful for it.

Without power, we had no access to things we're familiar with—things we've become dependent on without knowing how much. Without power in the kitchen, we couldn't prepare the food (okay, Joanne couldn't prepare the food) we were planning to feed our houseguests the next day. We didn't dare open the refrigerator or freezer, hoping that we could hold on to a little bit of the residual effect of the power we once had until we got power again. But sooner or later, when you're without power, things go bad, as some did for us.

Everyone has a story.

৵৽৹

But suppose I asked the question and I wasn't talking about electrical power. Suppose it was a spiritual question: how long were you without spiritual power? How long did you go in your life without Jesus, the Light of the world? How long did you try to get by in your world without the Holy Spirit to enable you to do the things you most need to do in life? How did you cope without the power of God when the storm clouds gathered, and darkness covered everything? How well did things work out for you, really, when all you had to work with was all the little insufficient makeshift substitutes lying around when you didn't have what you really needed?

And as your life without God's presence and power stretched on longer and longer, did you find that, no matter how careful you were (or thought you were), things just went bad?

Yes, we sure take our power for granted—until we lose it. But look how quickly our lives spiral down without it. And remember how the power coming on—whenever it does—draws out of us a spontaneous celebration of joy: "Yea, we've got power!"

My beloved brothers and sisters in Christ, each of us went for some time without spiritual power. Many around us are still without that power. We have every reason to celebrate the restoration of God's spiritual power to us. And we can help restore our neighbors' power, merely by telling them about how we got ours back. In other words: turn on the Light.

৵৽

20.

The Men's Chorus

10 July

Yes, there are pictures to prove that, on the first Sunday in July, several dozen fellows of our fellowship strode upon the stage of the O'Neal theatre (see footnote, page 34) in order to unite their voices in song as an act of worship to their God. Some of those who participated will not likely need the photographs to remember those remarkable moments, having been so traumatized by the effort of standing before the entire congregation and making music (of all things) that the experience will be forever seared into their psyches. All participants survived the presentation, I'm happy to report, as did the members of the congregation, apparently, who were in position to watch and hear the result of the near miraculous skills devoted to preparation by director Erin and accompanist Sandy.

You see—and please believe me when I say this, because I do so in complete sincerity—we did not just show up Sunday morning and decide to sing something together. We had actually practiced—several times—over several weeks—singing off the same sheet of music, so to speak, and in the same key, where possible, and more often than most of us probably thought possible when we started.

Rehearsals were great fun, and here's the surprise perhaps: The fun was not proportional to our musical abilities, but rather in spite of the absence of much ability. We made fun of ourselves and each other, without taking offense. We did (or tried to do when instructed) things that were strange and somewhat difficult for us to do (pronouncing letters and syllables a certain way, looking at the director, controlling our breathing, looking happy no matter what we were hearing come out of the mouth of the fellow standing next to us—or out of our own mouths) in order to improve our ability as a group to praise our God with pleasant sounds. We certainly wanted to sing the best we could when the time came, but we knew whatever we did would be good enough, on one level. (We were the *men's* chorus, after all!) So we didn't worry a lot about how well we were going to do.

It's kind of like living the Christian life. You come together with a bunch of other folks to worship God. Whatever your ability or lack thereof, you join the group, and spend time getting ready with people who can help you get better at what you're trying to do.

You find just being together a lot of fun—and trying to do things together, even more so. You know that you can't always do what you want to do for God as well as you would like to do it. But you always know that doing what you can, as well as you can, is all God wants, and that it will be acceptable to Him if you just do that. And so you're happy regardless.

And even the stuff that seems so traumatic to take on, turns out to be okay because you're all doing it together. When the moment of truth comes, God is helping your group give Him what He wants, and then blessing the effort with a special joy and exhilaration to overwhelm the stress of being over your head—or out of your range or key, so to speak.

And we *were* exhilarated when we were done with what we committed ourselves to doing—exhilarated by the fact that we actually did something wonderful together, and by the wonderfulness of the thing itself that was done.

Yes, there we were Sunday: out of our comfort zones, and loving every minute of it, knowing God was loving it even more.

So: like Men's Chorus—like the Christian life.

৵৽

21.

Housing Sacred Things

17 July

A year or so ago, one of the woodworkers in our congregation lovingly crafted a beautiful, inlay box and presented to the church. It was constructed to house sacred things.

Last month, we decided to move it to a more public place, and so for the past few weeks it has been fulfilling its purpose—to house sacred things—in a new way. On Sunday mornings now, we are placing it on one of the tables in the foyer of the school auditorium where we worship.

And the sacred things it houses now?

Prayer requests—your prayer requests. Beside the box is a stack of white cards and a pen, and a sign inviting you to write down your request, fold the card, and slip it through the narrow slot in the front of the box.

The cards are not sacred, of course; we print them up by the dozens. But the request expressed in the words you write on them are sacred because they are the deep desires of your heart that you are offering in faith and hope to God. A prayer request is itself a prayer, and as Paul points out in Romans 8:26-27, every effort to pray is partnered by the Holy Spirit Himself, to ensure that it is exactly what your prayer should say when God hears it.

In other words, your words on the prayer request card, like every other prayer you speak or think or feel or want to pray, become sacred by the grace of God accompanying them and transforming them—even the ones you slip into that beautiful box awaiting them as you approach our place of worship each Sunday.

And then, like the loaves and fish that Jesus multiplied to feed the multitude, your prayer request goes from the beautiful box to be miraculously multiplied as men and women in our fellowship join you in praying for the concern you have placed before God. Now, others place the desire of your heart before God in their prayers, which means they have united their hearts with yours. And their prayers, like yours, are sanctified and strengthened by the presence and power of the Holy Spirit delivering them directly to the heavenly throne of God.

The box is but one of the many beautiful things so many of you have given to God's service in the time since Trinity was created. All that you have given has become sacred to God because you offered them as sacrificial gifts with sincere hearts, just as you offer your prayers. But more beautiful even than the prayer box and all the other gifts combined are the beautiful containers God has crafted to house His sacred things.

I refer to you, of course. Paul wrote, *"...you yourselves are God's temple..."* (1 Corinthians 3:16, NIV). You have been lovingly crafted by your Creator to house the sacred desire of God's heart—the desire that you would desire to love Him and relate to Him—to communicate with Him, in prayer.

And so when you look at that beautiful box on Sunday as you enter our place of worship—when you place your prayer request inside it, know that in the place and time of worship, God will be placing the desire of His heart inside you. What a beautiful and sacred thing!

తుంరా

22.

Spiritually Sorting

14 August

There was a really big plastic bag sitting on the floor inside the door of the Ministry Center (see footnote, page 22) when I went in there for prayer yesterday morning. It was bulging with stuff. I took a closer look and discovered that it was crammed full of very colorful toys. It could have been Santa's bag, except I think that bag is made of red velvet and probably doesn't get packed till sometime in late December.

But being the clever fellow I pride myself on being, I surmised the bag in the Ministry Center was full of stuff being donated for Mother's Morning Out, which will start up right after Labor Day. We have a number of things we're hoping people will donate—including a refrigerator (but that, of course, will not fit in a plastic garbage bag).

Anyway, it turns out that I am not as clever as I pride myself on being (and I'm not the first person who has pointed that out). The toys in the bag were not things being donated to us; they were things already in our nursery that Lynn, our wonderful child-care leader, had carefully selected for us to give away. It seems that with the new opportunity coming to Trinity—with the growth we are soon to experience—it was necessary to clear away some of what we had been using to make room for new things we will need in the days ahead. Much of what Lynn selected had been used and enjoyed a lot, but it wouldn't be useful for us in the future, because it would all just take up space and get in the way of new things.

Whenever you bring something new into your home, you have to make room for it by doing something with what you're replacing. If you've downsized—or are planning to someday—making room is part of the process.

When you bring something new into your life, you also have to make room. You trade—hopefully appropriately and wisely—things of the past for things for the future.

It's a spiritual truth as well, and we're seeing it at Trinity. But instead of plastic bags of old toys, we're seeing old attitudes, habits, and perceptions being packed up to make room for new understandings, new commitments, new depths of faith. That's what happens when you experience genuine spiritual growth. The "new" doesn't just get dumped in with the old. The old ways are carefully examined and those that are no longer deemed helpful are discarded.

You want to make room for the new things God is giving you, and God is certainly giving new things. If you don't continually make room, there will be no place for the new and better things of God.

I, for one, find it hard to let anything go—even the useless things. But, oh, how life improves when you make room for the better things God is waiting to give you! If you can figure that much out, you really are clever—in the only way that matters.

ॐ

23.

Communion

This Sunday coming up will be a Communion Sunday. Of course, for those who attend the 9:00 service, *every* Sunday is Communion Sunday. But I want to talk mainly to those of you who attend the second service and receive Communion on the first Sunday of the month—this Sunday.

Ours is a most remarkable Communion[14] and I have been thinking a lot about it over the past several weeks. You're welcome to think about it along with me.

The first thing about Communion is all the different verbs we use to talk about it. I wrote in the first paragraph that we "receive"

---

[14] When we formed Trinity, most of our members were liturgical by tradition and were accustomed to "coming forward" for Communion. However, there was no place to kneel in the theatre where we worshipped—and it was too hard for many to climb the stairs to the stage. So we placed a tall round table on either side of the main floor, where we set up the bread and two chalices (one filled with wine and one with grape juice). Our members came forward and gathered around each table in groups of six to ten. The pastors distributed the bread to each person in the circle and then passed the chalices for each to dip his or her piece of bread. When all had been served, we all put our arms around each other and the pastor emeritus and I prayed a blessing over our respective groups (as you can see in the picture on the cover). Then those people returned to their seats and the next group took their places around the table. It was a powerful spiritual experience for members and guests alike.

Communion. Some say we "take" Communion or "share" Communion. Other people might ask how we "do" Communion.

But there are still more verbs you can use, which will also change and expand the meaning of "communion." For instance, John and Carol formally "joined" our communion last week in the second service—even though we did not "serve" Communion in that service. And I have been known to talk about "experiencing" our communion when I write to those who have been our guests in worship and fellowship.

The word "communion" itself is a combination of the prefix "com," which means "with," and the root word "union," which means "one" or "oneness." So the word "communion" means "with oneness," or to be "one with." We use the term "Communion" in the Christian church to refer to "the Lord's Supper" or "the Last Supper" or "the Eucharist" (a Greek word meaning "thanksgiving"), depending on our traditions. We usually mean the business with the bread and wine, but communion— being "one with"—can also mean the whole nature of our relationship with our Savior—and through Him, with one another as Christians.

And so, when we "take" the elements of Communion—the Bread and Wine—we "receive" them "with oneness"—oneness with Jesus Christ Himself, and oneness with each other. We receive the sacred gift of being "one with" God Himself. We "share" that gift. We are joined in oneness with Him. We experience that "one-with-God–ness." We "do" something that demonstrates that God has caused us to "be" something: individuals in communion with God and all others who commune with God.

And what I'm thinking is that you are in communion with the One Who commanded you to take Communion even when you are not standing at His table and receiving the elements and embracing and being embraced by those who are standing with you at that table. You are "in communion" wherever you are in the room because you are one with everyone who is receiving Communion and experiencing communion as long as the Communion is taking place.

So how do you continue to "receive" Communion and "share" communion and "experience" communion all the time before your turn comes to take your place at the table and then after the time you have stepped away from the table and returned to your seat? Every one of us is "doing" communion, "sharing" communion, "receiving" communion with God the entire time the Communion service is underway. The truth is, in the second service anyway, you will spend more time in the aisle waiting your turn or sitting in your seat while others encircle the tables than you will standing at the table yourself.

Have you thought about what you should do to remain in communion throughout the entire Communion? Daydreaming or chatting up your neighbor or fiddling with your purse or sneaking out early may not be the best answer. You could reread and reflect on the Creed or the prayers or the words of the hymns and what they mean in your life. You could pray your own private prayers of confession and thanksgiving. You could commune with your Lord as He has invited—commanded—you to do.

This Sunday is Communion Sunday. So commune—like you've never done before!

࿊

24.

A 9/11 Prayer

11 September

Today is the anniversary of the 9/11 attacks. I would like to offer a different sort of pastoral letter this week, in recognition of that day. I invite you to join me for a moment in remembrance and prayer.

❧

Let us remember those whose lives were taken from them in the midst of peaceful pursuits that day: men and women and children—of many nations, many faiths, going to work or boarding flights never to return, perhaps never to be found. Young and old, rich and poor, people like you and me, not perfect, but not guilty, either, of any crime worthy of their fate. Though we do not know, nor could we recall, the thousands of names they bore, let us remember at the very least that these were innocent victims of a hideous evil. Let us imagine the dreams they dreamed, the love they felt, the hopes they harbored deep inside. Let us mourn the accomplishments, modest and great, they will never achieve, and the holes in the fabric of our culture and country their absence leaves behind.

Let us pray: *Dear God, grant them Your peace.*

❧

Let us remember those who lived and died as heroes on that day: ordinary people—firemen, policemen, passengers on a hijacked plane—giving their lives for the chance to save the life of someone else. Let us remember that they represent the best of us, the quiet capacity for heroism that resides within us all. Let us remember that in the midst of hell these ordinary people rose up and became angels. They reached out, risked—and lost—their lives, helping total strangers and becoming in the process a light that shocked the darkness. They rescued innocent people and returned a nation's pride.

Let us remember the enormous gift they gave to all of us, with grace and courage reminding us of mankind's very best, amid its very worst.

Let us remember and pray: *Dear God, hallow their memory and reward their sacrifice.*

☜❀☞

Let us remember those who felt the fire and smelled the smoke and saw the carnage all around, who met death unannounced and face to face and walked away alive. Let us remember that they did not "escape;" they merely didn't die. Let us remember that they live each day "somewhere in between," bound to haunting memories they cannot put to rest.

Let us remember them on this their worse of days, and pray: *Dear God, heal the scars we cannot see, that torture nonetheless.*

☜❀☞

Let us remember those who lost without warning that day some irreplaceable person in their lives. Let us remember those who waited for the knock on the door that came with news that broke their hearts. Let us remember "the lucky ones" who put a coffin in a grave, and the others who must be content with a special name carved smooth and simple and deep into a polished stone.

Let us remember and pray: *Dear God, mend the hearts and console the grief of loved ones and of friends.*

❧

Let us remember those who rose up as the towers came down and determined "Never again!" Let us remember those who have taken a nation's answer to terror's evil plans and delivered it personally to the farthest corners of the globe. Let us remember those who brought the lightning bolt and the olive branch together hand in hand across the desert sands, who braved the battle line and now the assassin's bomb to change the world for good.

Let us remember our troops and pray: *Dear God, protect them every moment and grant them all success. Bring them home to those they love, safe and very soon.*

❧

Let us remember that the attacks a dozen years ago today were not directed against what we did or had not done, but against who we are, or better yet, the blessings we enjoy. Let us remember that they attacked what they hated, and in so doing, re-introduced a complacent people to this amazing country we love. Let us remember that more attacks may come, but no attack can destroy those cherished things we commit ourselves to preserve.

❧

Let us remember and pray: *Thank you, dear God, for all that You have given us in grace so undeserved: for the blessing of our nation and those who stand and lead—for binding us together as we face our vicious foe. Guide us in Your wisdom. Protect us with Your might. Forgive us in Your mercy. Fill us with Your love. Amen.*

❧

25.

Holy Compromise

25 September

There are a lot of inspiring things about out Trinity experience. I know this because I am inspired, and because many of you tell me you are inspired. Many of you are inspired by your experience of worship—which you would expect from a worship service. But, in our case, that's more remarkable than you think.

First of all, we worship in a place that was not designed for worship—a room that doesn't have pews or windows (stained-glass or otherwise)—a space where the floor slopes down and cold air pours down, especially on the people in the back. (We're planning to fix all that in our new building, by the way.) But you put up with it every week—to worship.

And many of you put up with elements of worship (or the absence of those elements) that aren't exactly what you would like. The majority of our congregation participates in a service that is our best effort to combine features of two very different worship styles. We know that almost nobody is completely happy or satisfied with the result—and yet you worship—and are often inspired.

That we are able and willing to worship together joyfully week after week in a spirit of holy compromise with each other is remarkable to me—and humbling—and inspiring. It says that the bonds of love within our fellowship and the strong sense of God's presence and blessing are more important to us than our personal preferences. Holy compromise is a sacrificial act—and you make that sacrifice every Sunday as you come and worship at Trinity. You offer your worship sacrifice, for each other and to God. And don't think God doesn't see it and value it for what it is.

One of those areas of compromise has to do with music. Some prefer more formal, traditional music. Others prefer more contemporary, emotionally expressive music. What you prefer is right for you. It is part of how you worship best.

Our preferences also play out in how we respond to special music. Some of us are inclined to clap when the choir concludes its anthem. Some of us have been taught clapping in church is inappropriate. Let me repeat: what you prefer is right for you.

But the anthems the past two Sundays and our response to them have suggested to me another possible holy compromise. Sunday before last, the choir sang a lovely, touching, reverent song. When they finished, there was a long moment of hushed silence, and then a few people clapped.

Last Sunday, the anthem was a rousing celebration of the glory and power of Jesus, our Messiah. When the music stopped, clapping broke out immediately and strongly—a spontaneous response to a rousing message in song.

Here's something for us to consider: the choir does not need our applause; they are not "performing" for us. They are leading us in worship and offering worship to God in song. So perhaps the music should determine the response. And different music might just call for different responses. We should be sensitive to the response the music calls for.

If the music is contemplative and draws us into a deeper sense of holiness before God, the proper response would probably be a reverent silence, in order to extend that sense of holiness into the parts of the service that follow.

On the other hand, if the music lifts our hearts and energizes our faith and stimulates our joy in Christ, then responding with the joyful noise of clapping would be a natural expression of what that kind of music was intended to do in us.

So here's the compromise: let the music decide. Don't clap just because you think you ought to. The choir will not be offended. And if the style or message of the anthem seems to call for it, people who want to clap are going to—go with it.

Sometimes the music will say "Let all mortal flesh keep silence!"[15] And at other times, it will be like the Preacher says, *"Whatsoever thy hand (or hands) findeth to do, do it with thy might"* (Ecclesiastes 9:10, KJV). Remember: God recognizes genuine heartfelt worship, however you do it. And I'm glad that's how we worship—genuinely—"heartfeltly"—together.

ॐॐ

---

[15] "Let All Mortal Flesh Keep Silence," French Christmas carol based on the 4th Century *Liturgy of St. James*, English translation by Gerard Moultrie, 1864.

26.

Tag Sale

2 October

Well, I've been watching our tag sale—excuse me, GIGANTIC TAG SALE!—come together for almost two months, and this afternoon from 4:00 to 7:00, a lot of us will drive down Highway 5 to a donated warehouse behind the Habitat for Humanity Store to take part in a different kind of mid-week fellowship and dinner. Today's the day for the members of Trinity to start the buying of all the incredible things the members of Trinity have donated. And what we don't buy, hundreds of other people will come and buy on Friday and Saturday. And thousands of dollars will be added to our building fund.

Some of our people have devoted almost every waking moment for the past two months to preparing for this tag sale—and probably some of their sleeping moments, too. God bless'em! People have planned, promoted, picked up, unpacked, positioned and priced, morning to night, day after day after day. What they've accomplished is remarkable!

What you and your friends and families have donated is remarkable, too. Now we need your help getting people to come to the warehouse and buy it all. Who can you call and say to, "Come have some fun and help us build our church"?

We also need you to help the people who come to shop. If you have free time on Friday or Saturday, please donate some of that, too. Watch what the helpers do today; that's the kind of help we need, for however much time you can spare, either day.

I confess that I didn't take the Tag Sale Class in seminary, so this has all been a real education for me. I've learned that you can have a lot of fun working very hard, especially if you are working together with other members of the church and all of you know what you're doing is really going to help the church.

I learned that all of us have stuff we don't need, and there's a real sense of joy in giving something to the church that will support its work—and the more valuable the gift, the greater the joy.

I learned that every member has different stuff. You can see it in the vast array and variety of donations. It's just as true of our spiritual gifts. All of you have contributed a lot more to Trinity than just what's in the warehouse, full as it is.

I think I'm going to learn before this tag sale is over that no matter how many wonderful blessings the church has to offer—just waiting to be claimed and taken home—every blessing has to actually be claimed. Somebody has to come and choose to make it his or her own.

It also looks as though whatever an individual may pay to claim one of these blessings, it won't be the full price. That has already been paid by someone else who has now made something of value available as a grace gift, which reminds us of the ultimate gift of grace that we have claimed at no expense to ourselves, because Another paid His all and gave us (for free) what He purchased.

Amazing what you can get out of a tag sale—if you hang around long enough—and watch with discerning eyes.

৵৽৽

27.

Halloween

30 October

Tonight, I am going to be talking about the history of Halloween. I don't want to give anything away early, but having selected Halloween as the subject, I've been thinking about the "holiday" in terms of my personal history. I've thought about my own experiences with Halloween as a child, the details of which grow in memory to mythic size and significance as my imagination enhances the reality retroactively.

I remember as a child how wonderful I thought it was that there was a day each year (in our case, a night) set aside for kids everywhere to go on a seemingly endless quest for free candy. An energetic, industrious kid of a certain age could fill multiple pillow cases with a broad array of generally nondescript sweets. Brand-name, bite-sized, safety-wrapped pieces were relatively rare where I came from, but no matter. Any kid dumping a mountain of goodies on his bed and methodically sorting it all into separate piles by categories from "YES!!!" to "Throw that junk away!" still had to be a supremely satisfied fan of Halloween.

So, that's my own personal "Norman Rockwell Halloween."

Today, of course, kids can't roam free all over town, or ring doorbells until the late show comes on. And even though everybody now gives out handfuls of the high-class stuff, every parent feels compelled to conduct a careful inspection of every piece before it's allowed to enter a kid's mouth. The "hauls" are generally smaller these days, for the reasons mentioned above. But even so, there are apparently parents out there applying arbitrary "rate of consumption" controls, even after the inspections are complete. It's enough to make you long for the "good old days" when the rule was: "Collect as much as you can; consume as fast as you want."

So can we "spiritualize" all this? Well, try this: In an always scary world, we as Christians are allowed to go out and ask for wonderful "goodies" (blessings) from God wherever we go (as in: *"Ask and [you] shall receive…"* John 16:24, KJV). We receive abundantly in the process, and everything we receive from God is the best stuff (as in: *"Now unto Him that is able to do exceeding abundantly above all that we ask or think…"* Ephesians 3:20, KJV).

At the same time, God (our heavenly Father), is watching over all of us in life, and protecting us even when we don't know when we need to be protected and what we need to be protected from (as in: *"But the Lord is faithful, Who shall establish you, and keep you from evil"* 2 Thessalonians 3:3, KJV).

At the time, my Halloween experiences seemed the stuff of sheer joy. I still have that same childlike delight when I recreate them in my imagination. But as I examine my Halloween behavior and circumstances rationally as a (relatively) responsible adult, I am appalled to think what could have happened to me. I can only conclude that I was being chaperoned and protected by a Parent I could not see. And upon further reflection, it would seem that my heavenly Father was looking after me the same way on every other day besides Halloween as well—which causes me to realize, as we approach another Halloween, that He has never stopped doing so—for me or for you.

৯৽৩

28.

Local Elections

6 November

Yesterday, we voted—some of us, anyway. It was a local election—the kind that turns out the yard signs and letters to the local paper, but spares us the months and months of round-the-clock TV ads and "robo" calls, and glossy mailers every day. Compared to choosing a president or senators or a governor, it's a "little" decision. It seems so little, so insignificant, that a lot of people don't bother making it. But as the saying goes, "Not to decide is to decide." And the smallest choice can have the biggest and most enduring impact. The local council can raise your taxes just like Congress can.

Life choices can work the same way. There are occasional big choices in life—the kind we pay attention to and just know they will transform our lives from that point on. And, then, there are all those seemingly insignificant choices we make every day, often without even noticing.

Or we don't choose, preferring to let the tide of life carry us along on its current, through and past that moment when a choice could be made. But looking back on my life, with some years now to reflect upon, I am astonished at how many of those mundane matters I saw as being of no importance at the time turned out to be just as critical in forming my life as any other. And as often as not, I did not actually "vote"—or decide. I just took the easy way out and let life happen—to me and around me. It turns out that life is made up in large measure of the accumulated consequences of all these infinite, insignificant choices.

Blow off your homework enough, and you blow off any hope of good grades—and the college you could have gone to and the career you could have had. Ignore the tell-tale signs of marital friction and you set up the destruction of your family and your home and your dreams for the future. Overlook enough medical warning signs and your health is destroyed and your physical life is put at risk.

In the same way, blow off your conscience long enough and you destroy your moral innocence and your ability to recognize right and wrong and, ultimately, your character. Ignore the spiritual disciplines of worship, prayer, Bible study and sacrificial service, and you set yourself up for the destruction of your soul. Overlook the presence of God in and around you, moment by moment, and you end up with a wasted, empty and failed life.

But God invites you to "vote" in every "election" of your life—to consider your options and choose every time—for Him. It may seem like nothing, but those of us who have been around a while know better. The Christian life is the recognition that it is often God Who is in the details, not the devil. It is God Who guides us, not just in the obvious "life-changers," but in all those little choices that don't seem to matter, but do.

I got a little paper badge yesterday that proclaims, "I voted!" God gives out a badge, too, for those who attend to their spiritual "voting." It says: *"Well done, good and faithful servant. You have been faithful over a little; I will set you over much"* (Matthew 25:21, RSV). It turns out that every day is "election day" in the kingdom of God.

കൊ൪

29.

Navigational Aids

13 November

Over my desk at home hang two posters, each one a picture collage of ancient nautical tools. One poster shows a collection of ornate compasses. The other is filled with spyglasses—handheld telescopes for scanning the sea. Both were essential in days gone by for mariners sailing vessels across the trackless waves. Today, global positioning by satellite makes the magnetic compass all but obsolete, and radar has relegated the spyglass to the role of decorative relic, a nostalgic nod to traditions of the past.

But as I think of what they represent, it occurs to me, we must still navigate by "compass and glass." The compass supplies direction, it points us faithfully in the way that we should go. We select a destination and chart a course, and the compass keeps us true.

The glass expands our vision, for we cannot see far beyond ourselves with the abilities we possess. And there are hazards along our way that we would do well to recognize—and early rather than late. And there is a goal for the journey we desperately want to glimpse. With the powerful aid of the glass, we recognize the hazards for what they are, and cast our eyes on marvelous things, great wonders to behold.

You and I are all on a journey together—an always glorious, sometimes daunting, journey. We are sailing together in this vessel the church, across the dark and uncertain sea of life, to a promised land, a distant harbor of joy and peace and safety that some will enter sooner than others, but all of us will reach in time.

And what do we need to make our way? A compass that points true and a glass that reveals to us a clear and far-reaching vision we could not make out otherwise.

The ancient compass still provides the true source of direction for the journey we must make. The modern means of directing ourselves all point another way. And the point of choosing a course to follow is to follow it faithfully home. A guide that deviates from what is true will destroy us in the end.

And modern ways of looking at life distort the view ahead. Only the ancient glass will spy out the one true Light.

We have found on this journey we are sharing together that God's Word comes alive. We read it together, regularly and extensively, because it tells us and shows us that it is God's compass for us, pointing us always in the way that we should go. We read the Bible together in faith and find that it clearly and faithfully shows us a true and glorious vision of our God—and the divine destination He's diligently prepared for us.

Compass and glass. Direction and vision.

And Trinity—where God's Word comes alive.

৵৽৽৻

30.

The Attitude of Gratitude

27 November

We are getting ready for Thanksgiving—traveling, cooking, gathering together with loved ones to mark a day dedicated to an attitude and an activity: being thankful and giving thanks.

The activity is the easy part, more people will pray over a meal tomorrow than over any other meal of the year. And that's only partly because it will be more of a meal than any other meal throughout the year. It just makes sense to offer a prayer of thanksgiving on Thanksgiving Day. We even provided you a Thanksgiving Prayer at church on Sunday, just in case you needed one this week. Giving thanks is a good activity to engage in.

But the activity should grow out of the attitude, which is actually more important. Think about the attitude of being thankful—or as one of my Navy Chaplain friends used to call it: "the attitude of gratitude."

Giving thanks because the calendar calls for it one day a year does not produce much gratitude. But an attitude of gratitude can motivate thanksgiving anytime—and all the time. An attitude of gratitude will also ensure that the activity of giving thanks is not perfunctory or fake, but genuine—a true expression of what's truly in your heart and mind.

Gratitude, the attitude, does more, in fact, than generate a lot of expressions of gratitude, the activity. The attitude of gratitude spills over into the development of other attitudes, attitudes that are essential to a happier, healthier, holier life. Gratitude also counters or undermines those negative attitudes that don't do anybody any good.

An attitude of gratitude works against the attitude of entitlement, the sense that you deserve what you have—and what you don't have, but want. And that entitlement attitude leads to other attitudes like selfishness, pride, condescension, envy, greed and bitterness. Without gratitude, what you have won't make you happy, and what you don't have will keep you from being happy with what you do have.

But when you recognize that you didn't have to have anything that you are blessed to have, you can and will be grateful for everything. And when you recognize that you do have what you could just as easily not have, an attitude of wonder develops at the gracious miracles that enable you to possess or enjoy anything.

Gratitude for what you do have nurtures the attitude of hope, the belief that you may someday have more of what you need and want. And hope is the attitude that makes all good things possible by opening you to the possibility of receiving them. Gratitude despite what you don't have moderates disappointment and cultivates a place in your heart and mind for a sense of inner, spiritual peace, which is the fertile seedbed of genuine joy.

As I contemplate Thanksgiving and the attitudes and activities related to it, I find myself being grateful to God for the ability to be grateful—to Him and to everybody else. And I think I will tell Him so.

How about you?

❧

31.

The Sacred Journey

18 December

This will be my last pastoral letter to you this year, due to Christmas and New Year's Day falling on Wednesdays. I wish all of you all the joy of Christmas. We love you and are honored and blessed to be on this sacred journey with you.

I wanted to reflect on this business of "sacred journey" with you for a moment. Life has long been referred to as a journey, and pop philosophers suggest that the meaning of life is found in the journey rather than the destination. But journeys that are long and arduous can become merely tedious and exhausting—even crushing—if the destination is not worthy of the exertion. For many of you, this year has been long and arduous—so, too, in some ways, has it been that for Trinity as a church. And that is why we must see the difference between life as a journey, and life as a *sacred* journey.

The journey of life becomes sacred—and therefore inspiring and intensely meaningful—when it is traveled with God and to God. Some of you have known for a long, long time that you were on a journey with God. Some of you have just discovered that God has been walking alongside you through your life, every step of the way. There is a deep and abiding confidence in those who are "old hands" at the sacred journey. There is a rich and wonderful exuberance welling up in those of you who are just realizing the truth about God's participation in your personal journey. Both are valuable benefits for Trinity in our shared journey. We are going with God, day by day, in the midst of everything we've experienced together.

And we are going to God. Some of our loved ones got all the way to the end of this sacred journey this year. They reached the destination. God has brought them to Himself. And we journey on to join them, each in our time. We journey on—with God—to God.

I see it like the sacred journey Luke talks about in the Christmas story, the story from which the only genuine joy of Christmas really comes. Listen to some of the verses you'll probably hear again in the coming week: *"And Joseph also went up from Galilee, out of the city of Nazareth, into Judaea, unto the city of David, which is called Bethlehem…with Mary his espoused wife, being great with child. And so it was, that, while they were there, the days were accomplished that she should be delivered. And she brought forth her firstborn son, and wrapped him in swaddling clothes, and laid him in a manger; because there was no room for them in the inn"* (Luke 2:4-7, KJV).

It is the ultimate sacred journey. Mary and Joseph are going about their business—doing what life demands of them—going, in this case, from Nazareth to Bethlehem. Mary is pregnant with Jesus—God Incarnate. They are on their journey with God.

When they get to the end of the journey, Jesus is born to them. They journeyed to Bethlehem—to God—to the place in their journey where they will meet God face to face. And notice that their sacred journey required riding on a donkey (or walking) for days when Mary was nine months pregnant only to find no room at the inn when they get there. Awful journey—or sacred journey?

And your life, with all its pains and sorrows, setbacks and uncertainties? And the life of our church, with our own recent difficulties figuring out just where and when we're going to be able to lay our burdens down?

The journey is still a sacred journey. We still journey with our loving God, every step. We still journey to our gracious God, Who has prepared a place for us in heaven—and for our fellowship, somewhere in town.

May all the joy of Christmas be yours on your sacred journey.

৵৽৵

32.

Growing

One week of the new year is already gone. Time flies—and faster, it seems, every year. But we have not wasted "the week that was." We have worshipped together and renewed our fellowship. We have met to study God's word together—picking up where we left off last year. We have been about God's business already this year—and will be about it throughout the year.

And what about this year ahead? I believe that God intends us to grow this year. I believe that God has made plans for you to grow, individually—to grow closer to Christ and deeper in your own personal faith.

I will be preaching this year on passages from the Bible that will focus on our growth as Christians and our growth as the Church. For a year, we looked at God's preparation for Christ. For a year, we looked at the presence of Christ. And for the next 11 months, we will look at what the coming of Christ produces—in you and in Trinity. I have to believe that this kind of extended attention to the Christian life will have a dramatic impact on anyone who is attending to God's Word throughout the process.

So ask yourself (and God) this question: "How am I going to grow as a Christian this year?" God knows the answer already, even if you don't. Or at least God knows all the possible answers to that question based on how you respond to all the initiatives He will take in His relationship with you this year. You don't know what is going to happen to you or those you love this year. It may be a delightful year or a very hard year, from your perspective. But it will certainly be a year in which God is actively at work in your life and your world.

In fact, you can break the question down further. Every day when you wake up you can ask the question: "How am I going to grow as a Christian today?" Ask that question and you are more likely to spend each day looking for the answer. And when you do that, the answer you will find will often (and perhaps always) be more miraculous and inspirational than you could imagine, come what may in the earthly events of that day.

Jesus said, *"Ask and it will be given you. Seek and you will find..."* (Matthew 7:7, RSV). If you pose the question, God will supply the answer.

Then ask the next question: "How will my growth as a Christian effect the growth of Trinity?" I do not believe that what God has planned for you this year is merely for your benefit alone. What God intends to do for and in you will strengthen the rest of us as well. Trinity grows as the individuals who are Trinity grow.

"How is Trinity going to grow as a church this year?" God knows the answer already, even if we don't. Or at least God knows all the possible answers to that question based on how we respond to all the initiatives He will take in His relationship with us this year.

It's going to be an incredible year, come what may, because when we ask the questions, God will reveal the answers and show us what He has planned for us. And, with God, to know is to grow.

ॐ

33.

A Symbol of Service

This past Sunday morning, Joanne and I found ourselves, not in our accustomed places with you at Trinity, but among the friendly but largely unfamiliar congregation in Norfolk, Virginia, where our daughter, Meredith, is a member. Two weeks (and a day) earlier, we were in this same church as I performed the wedding ceremony that joined Meredith to her new husband, Jeremy. We went back this weekend to participate in Meredith's ordination as a deacon. The members of her church had called her to this ministry, selecting her for a sacred responsibility she had not sought.

In the Southern Baptist tradition, new deacons are ordained for this ministry, which involves kneeling while previously ordained pastors and deacons (and, in her church's case, any members who wish) place their hands on the head of the individual and whisper prayers or words of blessing and encouragement. I confess that I was completely overcome with emotion when my turn came to place my hands on my daughter's head. God has now granted me the honor to baptize my child, perform her wedding and participate in her ordination—which, by the way, took place in the exact same spot where we stood for the wedding two weeks before.

But, believe it or not, what I really want to tell you about is what happened after the ordination was completed. As I sat down and "moistened the Kleenex" Joanne passed me, the pastor of the church made a presentation to each new deacon. He gave each of them—a hand towel. He gave them a towel as the most appropriate symbol of their sacred office—the office of servant. And then he preached a sermon from the 13th chapter of the Gospel of John where, before the Last Supper, Jesus took a towel and water and washed His disciples' feet. It was a good sermon— simple, succinct and strong—as are the words Jesus spoke when He finished doing a servant's work: *"I have given you an example, that you should also do as I have done to you."* (John 13:15, RSV).

What is a church, really? I think a truly authentic church is an association of servants, led by the greatest Servant of them all, Who served every other servant in the association first, by washing us clean of all the dirt that defiled us—at the cost of His honor and His dignity—and His life. He gave us eternal life at the cost of His own life—the only spotless life—and then taught us to live the life He gave us as servants—to live just like Him.

Not everybody can or will or should hold positions of high visibility, prestige or authority in a church. But every one of us can and should fill the position of servant—do the work of a servant. And if you cannot physically do the work of a servant, you can still seek to have the spirit of a servant. You can want to serve—value service—because you know that a servant's hand—and a servant's heart—are the closest imitation of the Servant that God sent to serve you.

And so the pastor gave them each—not a plaque—or a trophy—or a special badge—but a simple, everyday towel. And that's the way it works in the Church formed and led by our Servant Savior. True greatness in His Church it tied to the towel. And there's a towel waiting for every one of us.

❧

34.

Grieving Great Loss

22 January

Centuries ago, the prophet Isaiah wrote about a suffering servant—*"a man of sorrows, acquainted with grief..."* (Isaiah 52-53, RSV). Many of you are acquainted with grief—intimately acquainted. You have experienced personally the mind-numbing, heart-breaking, life-stopping grief of losing a beloved parent or partner or child. And for some of you, the experience is recent, and the pain undiminished.

In the past few days, we have become a fellowship of sorrows; we have suffered a great and collective loss. We are now acquainted with a common grief—undone by it in one way, and yet bound together more closely by it at the same time.

We have lost our beloved brother[16]: healthy, exuberant, engaging, and joyful one minute—and "gone" the next. An inspirational and highly visible leader of our congregation—a tireless and unsung worker behind the scenes—a man who loved Trinity with passion and believed in Trinity with conviction—absent from us now; but, thank God, present with the Lord. We are grieving for ourselves, both for what he has meant to us, and because this grief seeks out within us the other, individual griefs specific to each of us.

---

[16] The Chairman of our Church Council died in an accident in his 50s.

78

His wife, our beloved sister, has lost her life's partner and best friend, her fierce protector and greatest fan. And we grieve for her, for we know that hers is the greater grief by far. And yet we can imagine, at least, how she is suffering—and how she will.

And so we—this uniquely loving Christian family—will grieve. Grief cannot be avoided, once there is a legitimate reason for it. Avoid grief and it will come after you—with a vengeance. Grief will not be denied. Denials only serve to delay and deepen the grief that must, finally, be acknowledged and engaged.

The only way to get beyond grief is to go through it. We will go through this grief together. We have already begun to do so—together—in these past few days, through fervent prayer and searching the scripture and simple acts of kindness and comfort.

We will love and support our sister as she travels the long and lonely road of her particular grief, even as we have sought to support all of you who are on that road yourselves. There are no shortcuts—no alternate routes. Detours only make the journey more difficult.

But there is light in the darkness, even if it cannot yet be seen. It turns out that the suffering servant Isaiah described was and is, in fact, *THE* Suffering Servant, the Man of Sorrows Who has chosen to be acquainted, not just with His own grief, but with ours as well. He comes alongside us and shares our grief with total understanding and all sufficient grace. You never suffer—you never grieve—alone.

And because of Him, you never grieve without hope. With Him alongside, that long and lonely road actually goes somewhere worth going—and gets you there one day.

We cannot take away this grief, but we can share it and, simply by our presence, suggest the hope for healing that God will eventually cause to come to those who are grieving the most.

Our fellowship has been the source, for many of us, of a remarkable outpouring of divine, spiritual joy. We will now discover how God will strengthen the bonds of love among us even more, and pour out spiritual grace upon us more abundantly, as we share the grief of this tragedy.

God keep and comfort our sister—and all of us.

❧

35.

The Annual Meeting

12 February

This Sunday, after our second service, our membership will come together for Trinity Christian Fellowship's third Annual Meeting. We are required to hold an annual meeting by our Constitution and By-Laws (Article IV, Section 1), which means we imposed the requirement on ourselves. Or to put it more accurately: Those who were the members of Trinity in the first few months of our existence as a church fellowship "reached into the future" to require those of us who are members now to hold this meeting.

The first members of Trinity will also have placed that requirement on all those who will make up our membership next year, and five years from now, and 10, and 50, and for as long as there is a Trinity Christian Fellowship. It's not inconceivable that the time will come when none of the individuals who voted to require Trinity to have this meeting will be here to attend it. But it will be held, and the members of Trinity will attend it, because it is the required Annual Meeting of Trinity Christian Fellowship. It is in our Constitution and so it is part of what "constitutes" us as a congregation.

If all this sounds convoluted (and perhaps a little silly), let me draw your attention to an easily overlooked passage in the Book of

Deuteronomy. It's the first paragraph in Chapter 5, right before Moses repeats the Ten Commandments (first recorded in Exodus 20). The passage in Deuteronomy is part of Moses' farewell speech to God's Chosen People, given 40 years after they got their "Constitution" at Mount Sinai (also known as Mount Horeb). In fact, all the men who were 20 years or older during those months at Sinai are dead, except for Joshua and Caleb. Moses is talking to a whole new membership of the Chosen People.

And Moses says something very interesting: *"The LORD our God made a covenant with us in Horeb. Not with our fathers did the LORD make this covenant, but with us, who are all of us here alive today. The LORD spoke with you face to face at the mountain…"* (Deuteronomy 5:2-4, RSV). Our members wrote our Constitution and By-Laws; God wrote Israel's. But God made us His chosen people as Christians and as Trinity Christian Fellowship, just like He did those people He delivered from bondage and brought to Sinai.

God made a covenant with us at the Village Hall the night we voted to form this church. He made that covenant with all of you, whether you were there physically that night or not. He made that covenant that night with every person who will ever be a member of Trinity. Every person who will ever be a member of this covenant fellowship was face to face with God that night. That night, God spoke to you and to all the others, regardless of when you heard Him, or when others will hear Him. We may have written in our Constitution that we hold our Annual Meeting to hear reports, elect Council members and conduct other business, but God's purpose is to remind us that what He did that night was to constitute us, the members of Trinity, then and now and throughout the far-reaching future, as His Chosen People.

So, when you come to the meeting Sunday, remember: Whoever you are, you were there, when God spoke to His people—when He spoke to you.

❧

36.

Ministry

26 February

I have been especially impressed in the past few days by how so many of you are focusing on and embracing your individual ministries. A true church is made up of ministers. Every member is a minister—in the Name of Jesus, by the power of Jesus, for the gospel of Jesus. Jesus has given each of us the gift of a ministry so that all of us can enjoy doing what Jesus does by doing it with Him.

Now, here's where you might start thinking: "Guilt Trip Alert!" or "He's about to put the pressure on for people to volunteer for church committee work or some undesirable duty."

But think again. I don't "do" guilt trips (unless the Bible requires me to). My attitude is: If it's not your ministry, don't volunteer for it. We don't need miserable members dragging around the emotional ball and chain of a self-inflicted sense of moral obligation for something God hasn't assigned you. If it's somebody else's calling, let them do it. If nobody steps forward, maybe God doesn't want us to do it after all.

What I'm talking about is discovering that "thing," that when you think about it, and especially when you do it, just charges up your spiritual "battery" and you can't wait to do it again. What I'm talking about is the truth that every one of us has that "thing" God has given us to do that revs us up and makes us feel the power of the presence of God in and around us.

"Doing something" is not really the point. The point is realizing that there is something that is your particular, individual, ministry, whether you've figured out what it is yet or not. Jesus told His disciples in the Gospel of John, *"I have come that you might have life, and have it more abundantly"* (John 10:10, RSV). And later He said, *"whoever believes in me will also do the works that I do; and greater works than these will he do"* (John 14:12, ESV). To "have life" is to have received God's salvation. To "have life more abundantly" is to have received God's ministry. And when every Christian is engaged in his or her particular service for God, all of us together will certainly do more than Jesus did when He walked the earth, even on His most miraculous day of ministry.

But if you don't know He's given you a ministry, you might not be looking for it as you go about the routine business of your day. You might miss it even when it's right there in front of you. Or you might think, "I don't have a ministry; I can't do anything anymore." If you can't do anything anymore, perhaps your ministry now is *not* doing anything anymore. Ministry is not really, ultimately, about what you can do—but what God can do with you, even when He's doing it all and all you're doing is letting Him. The most amazing ministry takes place anyway when God is doing ministry in and through us and we're not getting in His way and trying to help Him too much.

So I celebrate all the ministry our Trinity family is engaged in—within our fellowship and beyond—seen and unseen—for the blessings the recipients are receiving, and for "the charge" you ministers are getting out of being ministers.

Enjoy!

⇛⇝

37.

Ash Wednesday

5 March

Well, Mardi Gras (French for "Fat Tuesday") is over. Today is Ash Wednesday.

Mardi Gras is "Fat Tuesday" because the day after it *is* Ash Wednesday. Traditionally, it is the last day before you enter into the season of Lent to "get IT out of your system." "IT," in this case, is carnival season: partying, splurging, overindulging, living off the "fat" of the land—doing all the things you shouldn't be doing anytime anyway because, starting with Ash Wednesday, you *really* shouldn't be doing them, according to Church tradition.

Starting on Ash Wednesday, Christians who observe the Lenten season are expected to restrain themselves from anything that smacks of the high-life. It is the season of self-denial that encourages you to turn your attention away from yourself and your personal desires—to Jesus, who denied Himself everything, including life itself, to provide everything, including eternal life, for you.

Somehow, at the stroke of midnight on a single day, the pendulum of human behavior is supposed to swing from one extreme on the spectrum to the other. In reality, it doesn't work that way. Year by year, Mardi Gras behavior becomes more and more "over the top"—or perhaps it would be better to say "beneath the bottom"—in terms of immoral activity. The more debauched and degenerate public Mardi Gras behavior becomes (let alone private behavior), the less likely the participants are to take part in any Lenten-like sacrificial behavior afterwards. It's just an excuse, and a cynically transparent one, to revel, and wallow, in the lowest form of human sinfulness.

If you wanted to spend the Lenten season getting closer to Jesus by acting more like Him in His life of sacrifice, you would want to use the time beforehand to get in shape for it. You wouldn't spend your time kicking up your heels on Fat Tuesday; you would spend the time bending your knees on Shrove Tuesday, the other name for the day before Ash Wednesday and Lent. "Shrove" is a form of the word "shrive," which means to "confess." And confession is a good way to start conditioning yourself for what you really want to accomplish during Lent.

It's kind of like getting ready for a long and arduous endeavor like running a marathon. You don't prepare yourself by bingeing on pizzas and popping bonbons all day. You train for the big effort by repeatedly practicing smaller versions of what you want to achieve—and avoiding everything else that makes meeting your goal more difficult…

…to which the world hung over from Mardi Gras today replies, "Where's the fun in self-sacrifice?"—assuming this to be an unanswerable question.

It's not. The answer is easy, and quick in coming. The "fun" is in celebrating the glorious victory in the race of life that self-denial, during Lent, and before and after, makes possible—that, and the spiritual help of the Savior Whose sacrifice for you you focus on in Lent. The "Mardi Gras spirit" just ensures that you will not be qualified to run the race with Jesus when the starter's gun goes off.

This afternoon, we share an Ash Wednesday service at O'Neal (see footnote, page 34). Mardi Gras is over. The season of Lent is upon us. So who's the loser—the one who passed on the party to prepare for the great prize—or the one who partied himself out of position and condition to participate in the great and ultimate race at all?

It's Ash Wednesday.

On your mark…

❧❦

38.

And Lent

Last week was Ash Wednesday, the first day of the Lenten season, and in last week's letter, I talked about beginning Lent. Well, it's still Lent, so I thought I would talk about Lent again. I don't intend to be "definitive" because there are various nuances in belief and practice among liturgical traditions—not to mention the non-liturgical traditions like mine, the Baptists, that don't even observe Lent (officially, anyway). What I would like to do is offer "an appreciation" of Lent by reflecting on some of the vocabulary most often associated with it.

There are some wonderful words related to Lent—words so full of meaning—so rich in inspirational power—that they are worth spending time with: saying them, thinking about them, doing them in our lives. These are words like "penance," and the related but different word "repentance." The Lenten vocabulary also contains words like "contrition," "confession," "self-discipline" or "self-sacrifice," "absolution," "fasting," "forgiveness" and "faith," as the latter applies to the rest in believing in their possibility and benefit.

But let me start with "penance," a part of the Lenten vocabulary that you may have to pull down off the shelf and dust off a little. We don't use it much anymore—it's gone out of style.

But "penance" is the appropriate attitude of Lent. It is focusing on the reality of your sinful nature and the significance of your accumulated sins. It is not wallowing in guilt, depression or despair. It is, rather, the willingness to take your own sin seriously.

Another meaning of "penance" is the things you do to demonstrate your regret or sorrow for your sins. "Penance," in the form of good deeds, "self-discipline" or "self-sacrifice" (such as "fasting") can't earn "forgiveness" (the victim's restoration of a relationship damaged by sin) or "absolution" (the removal of the moral responsibility to pay the penalty for sin). These are aspects of grace that, by their very nature, must be freely given. But "penance" can demonstrate the desire for "forgiveness" in practical ways, and may, to some degree, lessen the negative consequences of (or make some amends for) sins already committed.

"Repentance" is an essential part of "penance." It is the genuine change of mind that recognizes the wrongness of an act or thought. Similarly, "contrition" is a change of heart about having thought or done something sinful. In both cases, intellectually and emotionally, it is judging yourself according to God's standards instead of your own and accepting the verdict your attitude or action deserves. "Repentance" and "contrition" also demonstrate a desire for forgiveness.

"Confession" is the act of acknowledging the truth about your sin, which enables you to be "on the same page" with God about your words and thoughts and deeds that displease God and hurt others and yourself. It is the logical follow-on to "repentance" and "contrition," and is your opportunity to separate yourself, intellectually, emotionally and morally, from your sin.

If we are to make Lent our penitential season in preparation for experiencing the spiritual power of our Lord's Crucifixion and Resurrection next month, there is a language available to us— loaded with divine meaning—awaiting and supporting our "faith" in God's ability and willingness to draw us away from our sins and closer to Him. Even a Baptist like me can "appreciate" that.

•••

39.

In the Beginning...BANG!

19 March

There was an article in the paper yesterday about an incredible breakthrough in the scientific understanding of the origin of the universe. Let me quote a little of it—and sandwich in the kinds of thoughts I was having as I read it:

"Researchers say they have spotted evidence that a split-second after the Big Bang, the newly formed universe ballooned out at a pace so astonishing that it left behind ripples in the fabric of the cosmos."

In the beginning, God created the heavens and the earth.... And God said, "Let there be light," and **[BANG!]** *there was light* **(Genesis 1:1, 3, KJV).** (I added the part in brackets.)

The scientists made their discovery by scanning "about two percent of the sky for three years with a telescope at the South Pole, where the air is exceptionally dry."

The heavens declare the glory of God, and the sky above proclaims his handiwork **(Psalm 19:1, KJV)** (...even if you're only looking at two percent of it).

"If confirmed, experts said, the discovery would be a major advance in the understanding of the early universe. Although many scientists already believed that an initial, extremely rapid growth spurt happened, they have long sought the type of evidence cited in the new study."

[God] has made everything beautiful in its time. He has also set eternity in the human heart; yet no one can fathom what God has done from beginning to end. (Ecclesiastes 3:11, NIV).

"The discovery 'gives us a window on the universe at the very beginning,' when it was far less than one-trillionth of a second old…"

In the beginning was the Word, and the Word was with God, and the Word was God. He was in the beginning with God. All things were made through him, and without him was not anything made that was made (John 1:1-3, KJV).

"They were looking for a specific pattern in light waves within the faint microwave glow left over from the Big Bang…."

Yours [O God] is the day, Yours also the night; You have established the heavenly lights and the sun (Psalm 74:16, ESV).

"The researchers say the light-wave pattern was caused by gravitational waves, which are ripples in space and time. If verified, the new work would be the first detection of such waves from the birth of the universe, which have been called the first tremors of the Big Bang."

[God said,] *I will make the heavens tremble…* (Isaiah 13:13, RSV).

"One of the scientists was quoted as saying, '…nature is cooperating with us, laying out its cards in a way that we can see them.'"

…there is a God in heaven Who reveals mysteries, and He has made known…what will be in the latter days **(Daniel 2:28, RSV).**

I think it's wonderful what modern science *thinks* ("If confirmed…" "If verified…") it has discovered about *what* happened in "The Beginning" and *how* it happened. And perhaps modern science has.

But even more wonderful is to know already *Who* made "The Beginning" happen and *why*. And after reading the article, I thought:

O LORD, our Lord,
how majestic is Your Name in all the earth!
You have set Your glory above the heavens…
When I look at Your heavens…
   the moon and the stars,
            which You have set in place,
   what is man
      that You are mindful of him,
      and the son of man
      that You care for him?
Yet You have made him a little lower than the angels
         and crowned him with glory and honor
                        (Psalm 8:1-5, ESV).

That's news worth printing every day![17]

❧

---

[17] The article was in *The (Sandhills) Pilot*, Southern Pines, North Carolina.

40.

Third Anniversary

9 April

Tonight, we celebrate Trinity's third anniversary. Trinity Hall (see footnote, page 12) will be crowded tonight—it always is when we gather for our twice-a-year covered dish dinners, on our Anniversaries and Thanksgiving. And it should be crowded, because we have so much to celebrate—not just what God did in drawing us together to start with, but what He has been doing every day of the now more than one thousand days that we have been Trinity, His church.

Tonight is not a commemoration of a one-time event in the past. It is the acknowledgement of a milestone in an ongoing process of spiritual fellowship and formation. Tonight, we're going to talk about what God did and has been doing and is doing and will be doing. We will remember, and we will experience, and we will imagine.

Tonight is not about nostalgia for the founding because, even though the spirit of Trinity is very much the same as the remarkable reality we felt at our founding, the composition of our congregation has changed significantly. As we look at pictures during the serving time and dinner in a few hours, we will see faces of folks who are no longer with us. Some who contributed so much in the beginning have been led to other places of service. Some of our most beloved members have gone home to be with the Lord, and we helped them meet their Maker—their loving heavenly Father—with courage, faith and peace—as part of this fellowship.

And you will see new faces tonight—brothers and sisters who have joined us in the years and months and weeks since the spring of 2011, wonderful folks who have enriched our lives and our ministries and our church in immeasurable ways. We are so much stronger because of those who have united with us in love and faith in the course of our pilgrimage together. And even if there won't be much empty room in the room tonight, there is plenty of room for more folks to join us in the love and service of the Lord as members of the Trinity family.

And there are inspiring days ahead for all of us, for God is present and powerful in our midst.

సాంక

41.

The End of Lent

Six Wednesdays ago, we met in the theatre at O'Neal (see footnote, page 34) to be marked with ashes in the shape of a cross. Lent began—the season of spiritual and moral preparation for what we will experience this week—the communion of Maundy Thursday, the Crucifixion of Good Friday, and the Resurrection of Easter Sunday. The Bible begins the story of the Last Supper with the disciples of Jesus asking Him an interesting question: "Where will You have us prepare for You to eat the Passover?"

Let me break it down.

First, notice that the question is "Where?" not "How?" They do not ask "how," presumably, because they know how. They're grown-ups. They've done this every year for any number of years. They were taught how to do it as children. They know what preparation needs to be done.

But they are in a strange place, far from home. They don't know where they should make the appropriate preparations. They don't know where Jesus wants them to prepare. And so, they ask Him.

They do know that preparations must be made. They know that—as disciples—it is their job to make the preparations. And Jesus does not disagree with their assessment of their responsibility as His disciples. They must prepare for what He will do so that He may eat the Passover.

When they ask, He tells them where to go—and what to say when they get there—in order to be able to prepare for the timeless, traditional Passover meal that this year—with Jesus—will become the even more significant tradition of the Lord's Supper.

And Jesus tells them something else.

While they are concerned with where Jesus will eat the Passover, Jesus is focused on the fact that they will all eat the Passover together. And He has already made His preparations for that. He has gathered them to Himself.

And imagine being the person who is told, *"The Teacher says, '…I will keep the Passover at your house…'"* (Matthew 26:18, ESV).

And you should imagine it because that is what Jesus is saying: "Prepare for Me to come to your house—your heart—your life. Prepare for Communion with Me because I intend to eat the Passover—to share in Communion—with you. I'm going to share My Last Supper with you—and die on the Cross for you—and be raised from the dead for you."

God was preparing for all this since the beginning of time and we have been preparing ourselves over the past six weeks to experience the remarkable results of His preparations as powerfully as possible this year.

The season of Lent is coming to an end—the purpose for our preparations is upon us. Communion—Crucifixion—Resurrection. His experience—and us with Him—sharing and witnessing and worshipping.

৯৩∾৬

42.

Freedom

2 July

This Friday is the Fourth of July—the 238th Fourth of July (if I did the math right) since the signing of the Declaration of Independence on that day in 1776. On this date, we celebrate our independence and all that means in practical and psychological terms. And we commemorate the events that started the process that has resulted in the present realities we now celebrate.

In 1776, a remarkably small group of people signed a document claiming that all "our" people were completely independent of every bit of "their" government. But it wasn't "the country" that was declaring its independence. It was the people living in the country—or about a third of the people, to be more precise. Another third fought just as hard to avoid the kind of independence the declaration was declaring. And, as usual in things like this, another third of the people didn't care one way or the other and just wanted to be left alone, which they generally were not, as is also usual in things like this.

Those who declared their independence did not become independent—free—when they declared their independence. In one sense, their declaration did not make them free, which is why they had to fight a war. In another sense, they were free before they signed it because they were convinced they were already free.

In their minds—in their hearts—they were free men, whatever the politics of the day. To hear them tell it, it was their God, not the document they signed, that made them free.

As they saw it, a government does not make a person free—though it may claim to. A government does not grant a person liberty—though it may restrict or prevent the physical exercise of a person's—or every person's—liberty. True independence is dependent on individuals and whole populations realizing they are free—that they are at liberty to be the persons they desire to be—or think they should be. When people decide they are independent, no military force or political organization can alter the reality of that perception—whatever they do.

Unfortunately, while the people who signed the Declaration of Independence were declaring themselves independent—free—they were determined to reject the equally valid claim of millions of men and women living right beside them to that same freedom and independence. But that, too, would come in time—because God has set all people free.

The freedom we enjoy each day and celebrate this week is the gift of God—and of men and women who lived a long time ago—and all those who lived in freedom and preserved it in the years since. The freedom of the future will depend on what God and all the people in the past did—plus what God and we are doing now and will do in the days ahead. We have no control over what God does, though we may be thankful for that, since what God chooses to do is always better for genuine, healthy freedom than what we would have Him do. But what we do with our freedom is ours to decide—individually, and as groups, and as a nation. Let us pray that the freedom we bequeath to ourselves and our descendants in the future does not suffer from our stewardship of it in the present.

৯৽৽৶

99

43.

Disorientation

6 August

The carpenters and electricians are still hard at work in our office spaces, just like they were last week. These days, every day brings significant changes. Some, we merely observe; some happen to us; and some we initiate ourselves in order to control the change—somewhat. From the beginning of our existence as a church, we have made much of the fact that the physical circumstances of our fellowship have been temporary. And yet, we quickly got used to the places and processes of our worship, fellowship, administration and ministries. We became oriented to what became familiar.

For the next few months, we will experience disorientation. The familiar will fade away. It is doing so even as I write. The details of the future will take some time to become clear. New and greater demands will be forced upon many of us. While gaining things we greatly desire, we will lose things in which we have taken comfort.

At times, the disorientation will be physical: going to meetings in places where we never went to those meetings, finding a solid wall where a doorway used to be, reaching for a light switch that isn't there anymore.

The disorientation will also be psychological. Last week, I looked back at the empty room where I read, wrote, counseled and prayed for three years, and marveled to think that I would never work in that room again. Every day as we prepare to move into our new church home, we discover more things that will require us to adjust the way we worship, share fellowship, conduct education and carry out the routine business of the church—even if we don't know what those changes will look like in the end. The transition is, and will continue to be, exciting—and stressful.

When the comfort of orientation gives way to the stress of disorientation, we cope and console ourselves with the hope of the wonderful reorientation to come. We're upsetting the apple cart in the hope of making our way to a better orchard. And in the next few weeks, we will pack up our stuff here in our old place, and unpack it in another place—which will, by then, be our new place. We will move our meetings to a single building and, for the first time, be able to call that building—an actual church building— "Trinity." And in a few months, we will leave the familiar and sometimes frustrating facility at O'Neal (see footnote, page 34) for the sacred space at 425 Magnolia Road that will become familiar to us.

When I find myself thinking about—and dreading—all the work and change that lie ahead, I try to imagine what God is going to do with our congregation—which is the real church, of course, wherever we are—in this new-to-us facility. I imagine our first service and the tears of joy that will flow and the thrill that will well up within us. I imagine everyone's impulse to explore "our (Heavenly Father's) new house" and imprint details on our minds and hearts.

But I also imagine children not yet born, growing up in faith and knowing the Trinity building as the place where they met and learned to love God. I imagine older men and women coming to this area to retire and catching fire spiritually as they sit in worship, or study in a class, or make friends in fellowship, in that building—this year and next year and for generations to come.

Our move to the new facility will be like most of the "Trinity Experience": wonderful, but not easy. We'll be on our way soon, because God is on His way, and, as always, we have to follow Him to be with Him.

෧ඏ෴

44.

Moving

Today, the Sandhills Classical Christian School opened their preschool in what was, just several weeks ago, Trinity Christian Fellowship's Ministry Center (see footnote, page 22), Conference Room and pastors' studies. Just several weeks ago, their faculty and families were expecting to start a new school year in the familiar spaces in the Sandhills Alliance Church they had worked so hard to get ready. And then, without warning, they had to leave the old spaces behind and start over, racing the calendar and the clock, to get ready for today. What they have done is wonderful to behold.

This summer, our own Mother's Morning Out Program Director—with a little help from family and friends—put in many hours of intense labor, painting and redecorating the Mother's Morning Out spaces in the Ministry Center for the fall term that was to start in early September. What she accomplished was wonderful to behold.

And now she, too, will have to leave her hard work behind and start over in our new home, with only a few days to get everything ready for "opening day" after we "close," and the building is ours.

And because the Alliance Church has decided to rent most of the rest of "our" spaces while they wait for their new facility to be constructed, moving our offices, mid-week fellowship and Bible classes to our new building will be a good bit more cumbersome and challenging as well.

Moving into a new house is hard enough. Swapping houses with someone is a lot harder. And when house swapping involves three different "families," it is harder still.

Fortunately, all three of our families are related—through Jesus Christ. And so we endure the frustration, the extra work, and the uncertainty about what next month, next week or the next minute will bring. Anything "wasted"—from a worldly perspective—in terms of time, effort or resources, is not counted that way by God, Who has demonstrated in an incredible way that He is the Prime Mover in all that is going on with us—as in every other great spiritual transition.

Let me offer a simple psalm as something of a theme for us as we confront the challenges of "the great move" before us. The psalm is Psalm 126 (here, in the English Standard Version) and the historical context is the return of God's people from Exile to the home they had yearned for so long. The psalm begins:

> [1] *When the LORD restored the fortunes of Zion,*
> *we were like those who dream.*
> [2] *Then our mouth was filled with laughter,*
> *and our tongue with shouts of joy.*
> *Then they said among the nations,*
> *"The LORD has done great things for them."*
> [3] *The LORD has done great things for us;*
> *we are glad.*

No matter what it takes to make this upcoming move, and to make of our new home the most beautiful and functional place we can for our encounters with God, we know and will celebrate every aspect of it as "the great thing" the Lord has done for us.

And what of the "wasted" effort and frustrations along the way?

Look how Psalm 126 ends:

> *⁵ Those who sow in tears*
> *shall reap with shouts of joy!*
> *⁶ He who goes out weeping,*
> *bearing the seed for sowing,*
> *shall come home with shouts of joy,*
> *bringing his sheaves with him.*

Nothing we give as gifts to God—in time, talent, treasure—or "trouble"—will be lost in His eyes. All of it will remain precious—prized—in His sight. And for that reason, we rejoice. Everything will be rewarded, as we come home (to our new home He has given us) with shouts of joy.

ॐ

45.

Designing

Several days ago, Joanne and I stumbled across a documentary about Massimo and Lella Vignelli (pronounced "Vin-yelli").[18] I had never heard of them. Turns out they are world famous. And if you don't know who they are, you know their work. They came from Italy to America in 1957 and began doing what Massimo (who died in May of this year at age 83) said he wanted to do with his life: affect the lives of millions. For over 50 years, they were partners in marriage and partners in design.

Know that red and blue American Airlines logo with the eagle in the middle? They designed that. The Bloomingdales' logo with the looped "oo"? That was them. All the signs for the New York subway system? They did that, plus designing the layout for all the brochures in all the National Parks around the country. They designed homes and churches and just about everything else from chairs and tables to cups and saucers, with a lot of books and magazines and a line of clothing thrown in for good measure. Their creations are in museums around the world and serve as training aids in many university schools of art and architecture.

Massimo was the visionary and Lella was the pragmatist. They were a perfect team, loving and contentious at the same time. But

---

[18] *Design is One*, A Film by Kathy Brew and Roberto Guerra, 2012.

perhaps the most amazing thing about their remarkable work and enormous productivity was how few "tools" they kept in their "toolbox" to work with. When it came to graphic design, with hundreds of fonts to choose from, Massimo never worked with more than a half dozen, and usually came back to the same one (Helvetica) over and over. He always worked with a "grid," an underlying system of interlocking lines across a page that anchored everything visual in its proper place in a logical way. Lella's jewelry and architectural designs were also simple, sleek and very functional. The documentary was an hour and 15 minutes of stunning accomplishment. And like I said: I had no idea.

Last week, I began a study on Wednesday nights of great figures in the history of the church since the close of the New Testament era. I started with a group called the Apostolic Fathers (pronounced: "the Apostolic Fathers"). The truth is: almost nobody knows these guys. And yet, these were the guys who helped design the church we live and work in today. They collected and preserved the New Testament writings, exercised leadership over the young growing church after the original Apostles died, started working out key questions of the faith left unanswered by Peter, Paul and the others, and gave their lives as martyrs to strengthen the faith of their followers.

They and those who followed them in succeeding generations helped design our spiritual world. They affected the lives of millions—hundreds of millions—most of whom never knew who they were. They laid everything out on a trustworthy grid: the gospel of Jesus Christ. They kept coming back to one font—not a style of letters, but the Font of all wisdom, mercy and grace: Jesus Christ. They put their stamp on everything they came in contact with—a sleek, simple and enduring logo: the Cross. Though contentious for the message of salvation, they were remarkably loving of friend and foe alike. They were pragmatic visionaries.

And so are we. By God's grace, we are designing a Christian fellowship for ourselves and our community that is both simple and functional. The only tools we use are the ones God has put at our disposal. While grounded securely in our orthodox Christian heritage, we are looking for ways to live our lives into the future that are faithful to the Font, guided by God's "grid," and able to affect the lives of others, whether they know who we are or not.

Are we Vignelli? No, we're Trinity.

৵৽

46.

What's Going On?

22 October

Sometime last week, I bought a big calendar to go on the wall somewhere in the church so that we could write down all the different repair and renovation projects we are going to do—and when!—so that I can keep track of things. Right now, I can't.

Anyway, it's the kind of calendar that lets you write in the months and days and whatever else you want to put on it in dry-erase marker so that if something changes—like when the roofing work will start or where the painters will be painting next Thursday—you can erase what you wrote and write the right thing instead. And, yes, it's one of those "I'm not lying to you; the truth changed" things. Everything is subject to change around the church these days. I expect the information on the calendar will change every day as "plan encounters reality."

I want to know what's going on because a lot of you assume I know, and therefore ask me. And then I'm embarrassed to have to give you the "shoulder shrug salute."

I also want to know how things are progressing because I want our various ministry programs to know where they can meet week by week while various spaces go "offline." I want our staff and volunteers to know what's going on so they can begin their "creative adaptations" before the last minute. I want our staff members to know so they can be more efficient and less stressed. All this is to help us know what our plans are for using God's House.

And hard as it will be to get this calendar up and filled out and maintained up-to-the-minute, I suspect finding a way to help us know what God's plans for using us are will require more than paying attention to what's written in great detail on a calendar with an array of colorful markers. Is this a ridiculous comparison? The Bible calls us the *"Temple of the Holy Spirit"* (1 Corinthians 6:19-20, KJV).

Wouldn't it be nice if God would give us a calendar of all the important things He's scheduled to do in our lives to make us less like a building in need of serious attention and more like a facility transformed into something shiny and new? I could plan my day better if I knew that tomorrow God was going to work on my pride or my impatience, for instance—or that next week, God was going to strip me down to bare bones, spiritually, in order to build me up in Christ stronger than ever.

I probably wouldn't busy myself with some mindless distraction after breakfast if I knew that a definite miracle was scheduled for delivery on the doorstep of my life at that time. Sometimes it would nice to be able to check and see just what project God has undertaken in me, because I can't really tell what's going on from looking at what's going on.

But it seems that God does not work according to human calendars, even those that can be easily changed. Probably the best thing we can do is familiarize ourselves with the kind of work God does, reading the description of His repairs and renovations of people's lives in His holy Word. You may not know what God is doing at any particular moment, but you know what the end result will look like. You've seen His work in Christ's life—and experienced it in your own.

Even so, we'll still try to get the basics down on the calendar at the church. I need to know what's going on—and you may want to.

৵৹

47.

An All-Volunteer Force

12 November

I saw an interesting story in the newspaper yesterday: The last draftee in the Army just retired, 42 years after they "made" him come in. If I did the math right, he retired on his 62nd birthday, which is the mandatory retirement age, unless you're a general (which he was not). So, in essence, the government made him get in—and then made him get out. Like I said: interesting.

Now, the American military is truly an all-volunteer force. Of course, the shocking discovery many volunteers make after they come into the military is that once you've volunteered, it's no longer voluntary; you have to take orders, whether you like them or not. I spent 28 years on active duty as a Navy chaplain and had hundreds (if not thousands) of sailors and Marines come to me, in anger or despair, complaining that *"This* wasn't what I volunteered for!"

And I would have to tell them, "When you volunteered, you volunteered for 'this' and everything else you're told to do. You are legally obligated now to be obedient to everyone senior to you." This news, though true, was seldom comforting. But many who accepted this truth went on to serve long and illustrious careers in uniform, finding along the way that voluntary obedience was the primary pathway to leadership.

The church is also an all-volunteer force. Yes, there were times in history when folks were "drafted" into Christianity—or perhaps into "Christendom" would be the more accurate term—at the point of a sword or with other, similar inducements. But though Christ recruits vigorously, and has from the beginning, He never inducted anyone into the ranks of the redeemed against his or her will.

But if you do volunteer to become a Christian, as soon as you do, you discover that obedience is a bedrock value of a disciple of Christ. And assignments are frequently significant, calling for courage and commitment in their execution. We are all volunteers, Christian foot soldiers serving in the eternal, celestial army of God. Jesus says, *"Take My yoke upon you…"* which makes it sound like Christianity is all heavy lifting. But the Commander in Chief of Christianity also says, *"…learn from Me, for My yoke is easy and My burden is light…"* (Matthew 11:29-30, ESV). It's like the writer of Hebrews says, *"Although He was a Son, He learned obedience through what He suffered…"* (Hebrews 5:8, ESV).

If anyone was drafted into Christianity it was Christ Himself. He gave up everything in heaven to come to earth to undertake His essential service, and then gave up everything on earth to complete His assignment and fulfill His mission (Philippians 2:5-11). He refused to dodge the draft either at the throne of God or in the Garden of Gethsemane (Mark 14:32-36). As so we learn our obedience from watching Jesus being obedient. *"And being made perfect, He became the source of eternal salvation to all who obey Him…"* (Hebrews 5:9, ESV).

The last draftee in the American Army served 42 years and then was discharged. Fortunately for us, there is no mandatory retirement date for those who volunteer to follow Jesus. Jesus said, *"…whoever comes to Me I will never cast out"* (John 6:37, ESV).

That's what I signed up for!

৵৽৾

48.

Thanksfeeling Day

26 November

Tomorrow, in America, we celebrate Thanksgiving. Not "Thanksfeeling," by the way—Thanks-giving. The whole holiday came into existence because a small group of people had this core conviction that they needed to do something. And that "something" they knew they needed to "do" was giving thanks—to God.

There was no place in those days to go Christmas shopping, and still they gave thanks—or knew they should. There were no football games to watch and no TVs to watch them on, and still they gave thanks. In fact, because nobody's team lost, everybody was still able to give thanks.

There was a big meal—as big as they could make it—and they gave thanks for that, because they had known many days when there were only meagre meals—or no meals at all. They sat down to break bread with people they were thankful were not trying to break their heads. They gathered at great tables full of food on that Thanksgiving Day after gathering in graveyards for many months filling the ground with their loved ones and friends. And, despite their sorrow, they gave thanks.

Thanksgiving is now one of America's "shrinking" holidays. You may not have noticed that some holidays are shrinking—in the time, attention and energy devoted to them—and some are expanding. But it's true.

Halloween, for example, is a holiday that is expanding. What used to be a one-night event, with a few days devoted to gathering costume parts for the kids, has grown into a month-long exhibition of spooky lawn decorations, and another month before that of intense commercial marketing.

Christmas, of course, has expanded into the entire last third of the year, overwhelming Thanksgiving almost entirely and crowding Halloween for shelf space in retails stores all the way to early September. Valentine's Day has been expanding, too, though it is not an official holiday. Even so, the market for red hearts and "all things romantic" is oozing right up to New Year's Day.

On the other hand, Veteran's Day has shrunk, probably because it floats throughout the week and fewer people are veterans. Discoverers' and Presidents' Day (formerly Columbus Day and Washington's Birthday, respectively) have shrunk, except that they have now been drafted into the service of generic sales events.

And then there's Thanksgiving. It's obviously shrinking. There's just too little associated with this holiday to market. After you've bought the turkey and the dressing and some extra food, what else would you spend money on to commemorate Thanksgiving? And with reduced attention to the holiday, there comes reduced interest in its true purpose.

Will you give thanks to God on Thanksgiving? I'm not asking if you will feel thankful sometime tomorrow—or remind yourself that you should. I'm not asking if you or someone at the table will "say grace" before the eating begins, though you should certainly do that.

What I am asking is this: will there be a time on Thanksgiving Day when you consciously, intentionally, unhurriedly, physically, verbally give thanks to God? Will there be a time when you speak the right and appropriate words of gratitude and praise—when you name the good things that God has given you, or the bad things that God has prevented you from experiencing? Will you give thanks to the God Who is waiting to receive it?

ੰੰ

What's the big deal about *doing* as opposed to *feeling*? Surely, God knows I feel thankful.

The difference is this: feelings are personal—private. You can have them and experience them all by yourself. Feeling thankful is just about you.

Giving thanks is interactive—transactional. When you give thanks, you give it to someone else. When you give thanks to God, God gets to be involved—with you.

God knows that He deserves our thanks. He waits to see if we will approach Him to offer it to Him.

So, let me encourage you to spend the appropriate time tomorrow expanding your Thanksgiving holiday by giving God your thanks—as He would like you—and waits for you—to do.

ੰੰ

49.

Waiting in Advent

3 December

Advent snuck up on us this year. It started in November. I did remember, at the last minute on Sunday, to pull my purple tie off the rack and do it up so that I would match the purple stoles we wear at Advent. As I walked in the door at O'Neal (see footnote, page 34), I started worrying about whether the stoles were there in the vestry/sacristy/all-purpose storage room, but I found them (hiding behind the robes) without going beyond "Panic Level 2."

I thought everything was okay once I got "wired and robed up." But I got distracted at the start of the early service worrying about whether folks would know the lovely but relatively unfamiliar first hymn, and I completely forgot to light the Advent Candle. I stood right beside the Advent Wreath (with the candle lighter "gun" right there) for however long it took to preach the sermon and I never gave any of it a thought.

I guess I need to get some of those big poster sheets they use on TV to help comedians remember their jokes or let the audience know when to applaud, so somebody can hold up the one that says, "Light the Candle" or whatever, when I forget to do that or something else equally obvious.

After the service, when somebody gently pointed out my omission, I realized that everyone had been waiting for me to "let there be light"—throughout the whole worship experience.

Everybody was waiting…which is what Advent is all about. We are all waiting for Christmas and the coming of Christ. We celebrate His first coming—His birth as the baby Jesus in Bethlehem—at Christmas. And we start celebrating in these days leading up to it. We work very hard to "get in the Christmas spirit" prior to Christmas. And we have a lot of help—much of it at cross-purposes to Christianity—committed to getting us in the "holiday shopping spirit."

Of course, Advent is not just about waiting for the coming of the Baby Jesus. There were countless men and women of faith who waited over the course of thousands of years for His First Coming. We who have believed that this Baby Jesus grew up to become the Savior of the world—our Savior—with His Crucifixion and Resurrection—are waiting now with the multitudes of history for His Second Coming—His promised return in glory and power to close the curtain on all our history and usher the faithful into eternity with Him.

It is interesting that the Church's color for this waiting time is purple. The world bathes Christmas in red and green, white and silver and gold. Those colors make the season very festive. Purple is the color of penitence—of confession—of honestly acknowledging how desperate we were for this Savior to come in the first place. It is also the symbol of our fervent desire for Him to come again. Purple recognizes that in the midst of omissions and commissions, we wait for our Lord to come.

Advent is a time of waiting—but nobody wants to wait. And yet, a waiting time is also a time in which you can make the preparations, spiritually, you need to make to make yourself ready for the Savior when He comes.

God bless you as we share this Advent time together, awaiting our Lord's return.

৵৽৹

50.

God Bless All His Children

10 December

Monday and Tuesday, our Mother's Morning Out classes went on a musical field trip. They walked over to the Manor Care facility next door with their adult leaders to do a little Christmas caroling. Monday, it was the younger folks—the 15-months- to two-year-olds. Yesterday, the three- and four-year-olds made the long trek across the parking lot to bring some "comfort and joy" to our neighbors. And word had apparently gotten around after the first "concert" that this was an experience not to be missed, because the crowd that gathered the second day was much larger than before. The invitation has already been extended, and plans are already in the works, for regular return engagements.

I remember making those regular excursions to the nearby "nursing home" with the other kids in my church growing up—though we were older, by eight or ten years. Once every month or two, our teachers would pile us all into their cars on a Sunday evening and drive us down the street to a place whose name I don't remember, to visit with a lot of very old people I did not know. We took a stack of old hymnals and sang some familiar songs for them, songs that were probably a lot older than they were. And then we were encouraged to "visit" with the people—go individually and say hello to the folks who had come to see us.

When you're ten, 12 or 14 years old, going up to a stranger who seems ten times your age (and might also be hard of hearing or have difficulty seeing or be confined to a wheelchair), and trying to make pleasant conversation, is not really what you would most want to be doing. But when I was growing up, what I *wanted* to be doing never seemed to be a consideration when the adults in charge had decided what we all *should* be doing. And so, when the time came, we went, and we sang, and we "visited."

Was I "scarred for life" by these traumatic experiences to which I was periodically subjected? (After interacting with me for a while, you may surmise that I was certainly scarred by something!)

But, no. The truth is that the most significant impact "going to the nursing home" as a child had on me was to make me comfortable now as an adult going to see people in the hospital and rehab facilities and assisted living facilities and hospice. I am happy to come and be with you and your loved ones, to pray with you and console you and encourage you. I can "visit" with strangers I see along the way—with none of the dread I felt as a child—because I did it all as a child—and it was okay.

I remember one Christmas season, our adult leaders in church made us all memorize the Christmas story from Luke (Chapter 2, verses 1 through 20—in the King James Version, of course). I was called on to recite it at the nursing home for all the old people gathered around the room—and I got most of it right without too much prompting. And to this day, that is one of my most meaningful memories of Christmas.

Our little children took some wonderful Christmas presents to our neighbors at Manor Care this week. They took and gave as gifts their energy, their innocence, their curiosity, their guilelessness, their joy, their youth—and as many of the words to their songs as they could remember. And perhaps they can help us all remember that when we enter the kingdom of heaven (which we can only do by becoming little children like them) God will give us an endless supply of all those qualities, too.

God bless you and all His children, whatever age we are.

෨෧

51.

Christmas Eve

24 December

It's Christmas Eve. We "moderns" generally think of Christmas Eve as the day before Christmas. But in the land and time of the first Christmas, a day ended at sundown, when the light of that day gave way to darkness. One day ended as darkness fell upon it—and the next day—a new day—began—in that same darkness. In the land and time of the birth of Jesus, Christmas Eve was not the day before Christmas; it was the evening of Christmas—the beginning of Christmas.

All of my adult life, and perhaps earlier, I have sensed that Christmas truly began in the darkness of Christmas Eve. I have felt this, not because of the Christmas Eve services I have attended or conducted—and there have been many beautiful ones, as tonight's is certain to be. I have felt this way about Christmas, not because of the hype of the popular culture to get sentimental and spend money, or the excitement of putting out presents (or opening them early).

No, what I have come to recognize and look forward to is that at some point on Christmas Eve, everything that has to be done—or that we *think* has to be done—will have been done. At some point in the hours after darkness falls on this day, early or late, there will come a time when time itself will seem to come as close to stopping as it ever does in this life.

It may be as old, familiar carols are being played or sung in church, and blessed memories—or beautiful visions—well up within you. It may be as you drive home from a service or a get-together and you get to a place on the road where no one else seems to be out in the world. It may be when you open a door or a window, and the night outside is crisp and clean and unnaturally quiet. It may be just a few precious moments late in the night when there is nothing else you have to do, and you just sit there and breathe, and marvel that there is even a moment that doesn't seem to be rushing by like all the rest of the moments that make up your days—and have made up your life.

Every year, as Christmas begins—when the evening of Christmas is upon us—I have this sense that, when everything else is done and out of the way, I am closer to my Savior Jesus than I am at any other time, because all the things that get in the way are out of the way, at least for a moment, and—if I am lucky or fortunate or uniquely blessed—I will sense how very near God is to me—on this dark but holy night.

I hope that you will have that sense of God's presence—even if for only a moment—in the hours of the evening of Christmas tonight. I pray that your heart and mind can get away from the "Christmasness" of this world for just long enough to feel the timelessness of eternity and the proximity of Christ to you. I pray that nothing "modern"—nothing in this modern world or your modern perspective—will keep you from making a miraculous connection with your Christ tonight—during Christmas.

❧❧

52.

New Year—New Home

7 January

In a few hours, almost half our membership will bring food to our church and have dinner together. The tables were set up, and then set, yesterday, filling the fellowship hall and the foyer. I would describe it for you, but you'll want to see it for yourselves. Our hospitality team has planned carefully and worked long and hard so that all would be in readiness for our "Welcome Home" feast. I think it's going to be a wonderful and memorable time for all of us.

Our first Sunday in our new church is just days away. The "Sundays at O'Neal" (see footnote, page 34) part of our sign at the entry to our property has been replaced with one announcing the times of our three services. We've talked about having someone hang around the school this Sunday because someone will surely forget and drive out there out of habit.

It was a bittersweet experience this past Sunday after church to be loading our things, not into the crowded supply room or the stage wings for use the following Sunday, but into a moving van to be unloaded at our church, which was done yesterday.

When the prelude for the DayBreak service begins this Sunday morning at 8 o'clock, we will mark a remarkable milestone in the life of Trinity: for the first time ever, every aspect of our ministry

2313913232322122221

will be under one roof—and the only space we will be renting will be off-site storage. Doesn't it just make you want to stand up and sing "Praise God from Whom all blessings flow!"—even if you can't sing.

There will be some singing tonight as we preview one of the songs the folks in our NewSong service—our first NewSong service—will be singing. We'll also sing "Happy Birthday"—as we always do—and celebrate a few anniversaries, too. After that, we'll talk some about how we all can help make this Sunday a superb kick-off Sunday.

Sunday is going to be very exciting for all of us, but we all need to be focused on things like safety (for instance, being careful navigating the broken and uneven sidewalks leading up to the main entrance—and holding the rails going up or down the stairs inside the church because the steps are a little steeper than you might expect); and things like "church etiquette" (such as, maybe you should move in to the middle of your row when you arrive, if the seats there are empty—and if you need to get to your seat after the service has already started, wait until the congregation is standing and singing to come in and go to your seat, or take an empty seat in back). Every one of us should be thinking this Sunday like hosts and hostesses rather than guests. We should be "eyes open" for people who need help or direction, or those who just seem alone. We are all the advertisement for Trinity.

But even being on our best behavior won't diminish this watershed event for us. The Lord has been with us—and is with us—and will be with us and for us in the future. We're ready for that future—that future that begins with the present. And, as I said, I hope you can be a part of our delightful dinner today and our wonderful worship this Sunday. The future is coming.

❧

53.

First Sunday

14 January

Let's "recap" the past seven days. Over a hundred of you showed up for dinner last week—and brought food—and everybody still got a place to sit (whether in the fellowship hall or the foyer or the music room), with only minor delays. And everyone got to eat and enjoy a great night of fun and friendship together.

Sunday, we launched our three worship service/two Sunday School/one fellowship schedule with more people in every service than expected. More people showed up for the slightly abbreviated Daybreak service than usually attend it, even though it met an hour earlier than usual. The first NewSong service saw forty percent more people than my optimistic expectation for its inaugural attendance. Half the seats on the main level had people in them. And the Cornerstone service still filled 80 percent of our total seating capacity, upstairs and down—on our first Sunday in our new home.

Several of our Sunday School classes will have to be moved to larger rooms this Sunday because too many of you showed up to fit comfortably where we had your class assigned. The changes will affect both adults and children, so stay tuned for details.

We were fortunate that the Fire Marshall did not drop in for a visit during our Fellowship time—and not just because we ran out of donuts! Traffic flow between 10:15 and 10:30 got "a bit interesting," and we're already working on how to provide more room so that we don't suffer from gridlock waiting to get into the sanctuary for the Cornerstone service.

Sunday was a glorious day for Trinity, but there are still a lot of things for us to adjust and improve. Some of them we saw. Some of them, you will have to point out to us. We're meeting later today with our Worship Committee members to get their assessments. We'll be talking around our dinner tables tonight with 60 or so about what we did right—and wrong—last Wednesday and Sunday. And we invite you to provide your own feedback, even if you can't be with us tonight. What did you see, hear or experience that we should know? Send us an email or write the details down on a piece of paper. Let us know what you think.

Of course, we could fix just about everything if we just had more room. But the building constrains us, as we knew it would, even as we moved our Sunday program into it. And it will be some time before more space can be provided, though we should not be fainthearted looking into the future, given what we have seen God do, for us and in us, in our past.

But it was good to get a sense of the vibrancy and the strength and the joy of Trinity as we finally "came home" this week. It was right for us to celebrate, even if we had to do our celebrating in close quarters. Just think how many churches would love to have the "problems" we encountered this week.

And, of course, God has given us these "problems" as a gracious and benevolent answer to our prayers over the past four years—prayers for spiritual power and a loving fellowship—prayers for a life-changing relationship with Jesus for each of us, and a world-changing impact for our church.

"Be careful what you pray for," since even the good things of God can challenge your ability to cope with the consequences of His grace. But, by all means, keep praying! God is just beginning to be generous.

And to recap: It sure is good to be home.

སྲོ‑ᡒ

54.

The Church God is Working On

I wanted to take a week off from writing about the church we are working on and think with you about the church God is working on. It is so easy for us to be focused—even fixated—on all that we have done—or all that we still have to do—to the building and grounds we purchased.

But as I said way back when you added "senior" to my title, when we acquire a building of our own, it will not be a church, it will merely be a "facility"—a resource to facilitate the life and work of what is really the church: us.

We refer to the building as our "church" because it is convenient to do so, but we should not be confused in our minds about the truth. Our church is the community formed by the Holy Spirit in binding us together in response to our individual faith in Jesus and our desire to be part of this remarkable family, moving through this life on the way to the next, in the company of our Christ and each other.

That being said, I find my thoughts going back to the building and the many different details involved in the process of its renovation. So let's compromise: I'll talk about some specific aspects of the building and try to use these things as springboards for spiritual thoughts.

For instance, for the first time since I started preaching to you as Trinity, some of you are sitting in a balcony. You are right there in front of me—in plain view—and yet I am so used to preaching to a "grounded" congregation, I have to remember to look up as I deliver the sermon.

Now consider what I just said from a spiritual perspective: "I have to remember to look up as I deliver the sermon." And to shorten the image further: "Look up as I deliver the sermon." I hope that as I preach each Sunday, I remind you to "look up." If you are listening to a sermon and not being reminded to look up, remind yourself—and not just to look up to the balcony level. Look up to heaven—to God. As your ears listen to what a man is saying, let your heart and spirit listen for what God is saying to you through whatever I'm saying.

And speaking of listening, many of you have commented how much better the acoustics are in our facility as compare with the theatre at O'Neal (see footnote, page 34). Some of that change is the superb sound system that has been installed in the sanctuary (and throughout the building). Some of the improvement is a factor of the smaller size and different design of the room. Is it possible that we all could hear God better if we reduced the distance between Him and us, and redesigned the environment where He would speak to us, and put better systems in place to transmit His Word to us?

Most people are delighted with the new chairs (though I did hear an N.C. State fan grouse a little).[19] Not only does the vibrant color please most of us, the ability of the chairs to connect to one another and turn in toward one another is also appealing.

In the same way, your spiritual vibrancy is very attractive—even to strangers who visit us. And you are not isolated individuals who happened to be lined up in the same place. All we have been

---

[19] The chairs are covered in a beautiful blue fabric (pleasing to UNC and perhaps even Duke fans). N.C. State colors are red and black.

through together has joined us securely to one other, and what we have shared and are sharing of our joys and (especially) our sorrows, draws our hearts toward one another in compassion and commitment. Someone has already discovered that if you try to jerk our chairs apart, you can damage them. The same is true of our fellowship. When a connection frays, we want to gently restore and strengthen it.

I suspect God has built a lot more spiritual insights for our church into our new facility, and our renovations of it. Let me know what you discover.

৯৩৬

55.

The Message of Christian Martyrs

18 February

Today is an unusual Ash Wednesday. Yesterday, we kept the church office closed because of the ice, and cancelled a full day of activities to keep our people safe. This morning, we have been glued to the weather forecasts again, to see if it will be any safer for us to hold our Ash Wednesday service tonight. What we have seen is that it will be dry throughout the course of the day, but that the temperatures combined with the winds will keep the wind chill factor at or below freezing all day, and that a light snow may begin falling during the time we would be in the service. And though they have been out plowing the roads, we can't guarantee that moisture on our parking lot, or portions of it, won't be frozen again.

So, we will not hold our Ash Wednesday service as scheduled tonight.

That being said, I suppose this becomes my only opportunity to share my Ash Wednesday message with you. And if you can't imagine Ash Wednesday without receiving an imposition of ashes, perhaps after you have read this letter, you could print it out, burn the paper in a bowl, add a little olive oil to the residue to give it some cohesiveness, and apply your own Lenten mark on your forehead or hand. It's sort of an "Ash Wednesday meets Mission Impossible" idea.

Leaving the weak attempt at levity aside, acknowledging Ash Wednesday is a worthwhile activity. And if we cannot begin the Lenten season together physically, it would still be good to take the time individually to remember that today begins 40 days (the Sundays aren't included in the calculation) during which a good part of the Christian Church will turn its attention to the sacrifice Christ made on the Cross for us and our redemption. Lent is the "Let's not take His sacrifice for granted" season.

This need to "return to the Cross" has been brought home to me forcefully in recent days as we have watched other Christians, dressed up in orange coveralls and lined up along a beach, have their lives taken from them because they gave those lives to Christ. In a way, they, too, have died for all of us—not to provide any form of salvation, something only Christ could do—but to remind us that it is in losing our lives for His sake that we gain them (Matthew 10:39), whether we give them up metaphorically or physically.

What happened to our Christian brothers reminds us in a visceral way of what happened to Christ—and reminds us as well that our Christian faith is not a philosophy of preferred behavior and beliefs. It is a complete reversal of our eternal fate, from condemnation to full pardon and reconciliation with God. And for that reason, we live a life of daily cross-bearing in order to be in fellowship with the One Who bore His Cross to Calvary for us.

In the scriptures we were to have read tonight (Genesis 28:10-17), Jacob wakes up after a night in the wilderness, having dreamed of heaven and realizing God had been right there with him and he didn't know it. In the gospel (Matthew 26:36-44), Jesus knows God is there with Him in the Garden of Gethsemane even as His friends and followers sleep. God promises Jacob a great life and Jesus promises God He will give up His life if God wants it so. And give it He does, with all that means for our lives, now and forever.

Perhaps Ash Wednesday is the day we determine to wake up to the nearness of God in the suffering of His Son for us—and remember that the life of promise God has given us was made possible by Jesus giving up His life as He promised God He would do.

৯৩

56.

Snow

Except for the part about it being Ash Wednesday, I could reuse the first paragraph of last week's letter, word for word, today. The coming snow storm has forced us to cancel our evening program—again!

There is something dramatic about seeing "HEAVY SNOW" in all capital letters with a big, red exclamation point beside it on the hour-by-hour forecast on the computer. So we're supposed to see a lot of snow falling tonight. And the mental image called to mind God's question to Job in Chapter 38: *"Have you entered the storehouses of the snow?"* (Job 38:22, ESV).

Of course, ancient folks didn't understand the scientific intricacies of meteorology—the cycle of evaporation and condensation and changes in barometric pressures—that propel the constant parade of "weather." But temperature and precipitation had a far greater impact on the biblical world of primitive farming and shepherding than they do on ours. And those people understood—or should have—that they were at the mercy of the weather—and the One Who created it and controls it.

The entire Book of Job is an effort to understand an individual's relationship with the God Who creates and controls the weather and everything else (see Elihu's majestic summary of God's power in Chapter 37). And by the time they get to Chapter 38, where God finally appears to Job and speaks to him out of the whirlwind, the distinction between God and man is clear: God is God and man is not.

"Where were you when I laid the foundation of the earth?"
"Have you commanded the morning since your days began?"
"Have the gates of death been revealed to you?"
"Have you entered the storehouses of the snow?"

Perhaps, when we wake up in the morning, we will feel like we have entered "the storehouses of the snow," though what we may see will be nothing compared to what many of you routinely experienced where you lived before you moved to North Carolina to get away from harsh winter weather. Whatever falls out of the sky tonight will be a reminder (if we allow it to be) of the sovereignty of God over the world and the people He created.

Like its Creator, snow can be beautiful and powerful and beneficial and dangerous, all at the same time. You can sweep it or shovel it off your driveway or roll it into balls, but you cannot make it fall when you want it to (like on Christmas Eve, for instance), or make it stop when you've had enough (like now).

And for all our modern, superior knowledge about the creation of snow, we have no more "entered its storehouses" than Job had. But perhaps, if we are listening with the ears of our hearts, we may hear the voice of God in things like snow, just as Job heard it in the whirlwind. Perhaps, if we look with the eyes of faith, we will see God's hand at work—even tonight.

అ•ఇ

57.

A (Spiritual) Music Review

4 March

Monday evening, Joanne and I were attending a glorious concert. A friend had generously provided us tickets as a gift, and we sat and listened, enraptured, to Vivaldi's "The Four Seasons," a set of four very famous violin concertos composed almost three hundred years ago.

On stage were the 15 members of East Carolina University's superb Four Seasons Chamber Orchestra (two of whom are "local girls" and related to two of our Trinity members). There were violins, violas, cellos, a bass violin and a harpsichord in supporting roles. In addition, there were four solo violinists who "rotated" in and out of the spotlight at center stage, each taking the lead, in turn, for one of the "seasonal" sessions.

And interspersed between the very familiar Vivaldi "Seasons," were four pieces by a 20th Century Argentinian composer named Astor Piazzolli, entitled "The Four Seasons of Buenos Aires." (No, I had never heard of him—or them—either.) These pieces were completely unfamiliar and very different from the well-known Vivaldi melodies. Yet in their own non-classical way, they were complementary and equally captivating.

So, am I writing a concert review, or what? No, I want to draw some insights for Trinity from this "outside the (church) box" experience, such as: Not everybody got a chance to step into the spotlight, but everybody played his or her best, and by doing so, enabled the soloist of the moment to have the greatest impact. Even the solo part—as beautiful as it was—was still, finally, a *part* of the overall ensemble.

No one—no matter how gifted—stayed in the spotlight forever. When one soloist's responsibility was completed, the limelight was voluntarily relinquished so that the next could step forward and the concert could proceed.

And proceed it did. There was no intermission—no interruption or long delay in the process. Once everyone had shifted positions, taken a breath, and the instruments were retuned, they were off again, making more beautiful music together.

And when each soloist was not in the spotlight (which was three-fourths of the time), he or she joined the supporting ensemble, playing a subordinate role with as much dedication as he or she had displayed as the featured performer. In fact, *everyone* shifted when the soloists changed, which they did as the "seasons" changed, so that every member of the ensemble had the opportunity to play both lesser and greater parts in support throughout the course of the whole performance. On several occasions, members of the ensemble even had solo parts that formed a counterpoint to themes the official soloists were playing.

Sometimes, what we heard were the familiar and beloved melodies that comforted us (Vivaldi). But before long, we would be subjected to new sounds—new themes—that surprised us and fascinated us and challenged us with their energy and inventiveness (Piazzolli). And as the performance went on, we began to sense how the classic work and the contemporary work were interwoven to form a unified and enriching whole that we had not anticipated when the program began.

And I learned later that all the performers went from the concert to a large lovely home afterward for a reception, an opportunity to celebrate and be properly praised for what they had accomplished together.

છ્ન્લ

Trinity is a spiritual ensemble, formed by God's Holy Spirit to play both old and new melodies of faith that God has composed for us. We play different parts with different instruments as God has made us able and directed us. At times, we play subordinate, supportive parts. Occasionally, our part may bring us into the spotlight. We want to play our best, and we play our best when we play together, as an ensemble. God has made it possible for us both to play beautifully and to play what is beautiful. And He has prepared a glorious reception in a wonderful home when the concert is over to celebrate and praise us for our performance of His special composition consisting of the seasons of life.

It was wonderful to be there listening to the beautiful music Monday night. I have to believe it was even better to be there making it. Thank God for the music He is making with us.

છ્ન્લ

58.

B.C, A.D., Etc.

11 March

In our Bible study class yesterday, we got to talking about dates and calendars and this whole "B.C."—"A.D." business, which can be so confusing, since the "B.C." numbers go "backwards." The conversation continued after class was dismissed, so some of you who were in the class—and all of you who weren't—will have missed what was said.

When we put "A.D." or "B.C." after a date, it can be confusing or misleading if you don't understand the process (and very informative if you do). "B.C." is the easy part. It means "Before Christ"—and measures time from the day before Jesus was born "back" in time. More on that in a minute.

Since the "B" stands for "Before," a lot of English-speaking people assume the "A" stands for the opposite of "B"—"After"—and guess the "D" means "Death," as the opposite of His birth, which they understand is when "B.C." starts. But "After Death" leaves 30 to 33 years unaccounted for—a pretty important three decades in the history of things.

It turns out that "A.D." doesn't actually mean "After Death." It's not even English, in fact. It abbreviates a Latin phrase, which is the language everybody was using in the European church five hundred years after the earthly life of Jesus, which is when the Christian calendar and the phrase were invented.

"A.D." means "Anno Domini." "Anno" means "in the *year* (think 'annual')" And "Domini" means "of our *Lord*." Although the medieval churchmen were off by a few years in their calculations, the intention was to start numbering years (backward and forward) from the birth of Christ—the most important event in history. So, 1 A.D. (theoretically) began the day Jesus was born—and 1 B.C. began the day before that. There is no "Year 0," A.D. or B.C., in this system.

So why do they do "B.C." dates "backward"? Well, both "A.D." and "B.C." "measure" how far away in time from the birth of Christ something else happened. It's like mileage in different directions. If you were traveling *distance* instead of *time*, the miles would add "up" the farther away from your starting point you got, regardless of the direction you were going.

Suppose St. Louis was your starting point. Whether you were going to Washington, D.C., or San Francisco, the farther from St. Louis you went in either direction, the larger the number of miles you traveled would be. A thousand years before the birth of Christ is the same "distance" away from His birth as a thousand years after, just like you're as far away from St. Louis if you've gone a thousand miles west as you would be if you have gone a thousand miles east. You're just measuring the distance from one particular place.

It took the church till about 800 A.D., to get everybody in Christendom on board with this dating system, and now everybody in the world uses it.

But not everybody who has to use it is Christian, so over the past few centuries—and especially in the last one—non-Christians (and Christians who wanted to communicate with them without giving offense) began using "neutral" phrases to refer to the two side of the "birth of Jesus divide." The standard secular terms now are "C.E." (for "Common Era") in place of "A.D.," and "B.C.E." (for "Before the Common Era") for "B.C."

Of course, it'll always be good old "B.C." and "A.D." to me: good enough for God—good enough for me.

God bless you, in this year of our Lord.

❧

59.

New Flowers

We found some new flowers at home in the back yard today. They were "new" in the sense that spring is here and new flowers flowering is what happens right about now—they had just started blossoming. But more than that, they were "new" because we had never noticed them growing there before. And we've had the same back yard with the same big bush for a number of years now. Funny how we must have looked at them so many times before and never looked closely enough to realize they were flowers—and beautiful ones at that.

The truth is that I didn't notice them *this* time; Joanne pointed them out to me. She had cut some and brought them inside to put in an arrangement with some of the other flowers that grow in the yard that I have seen. And she hadn't really noticed these new flowers herself, she said, until the fellow who does our yard work pointed them out to her. He knows back yard flowers better than we do, I guess, as he should.

But I don't feel so bad about not noticing them because it turns out these flowers are very, very small. They're like miniature flowers. You almost need a magnifying glass to appreciate their elegant beauty. You certainly have to get up close to see the delicate detail. But when I finally saw what had been there all the time (even though I had never seen it), I was captivated by the beauty, and fascinated that something so wonderful had been right there where I live, all the time. Small flower—big impact.

And now for the analogy.

৯৵৯

The blessed Word of God is blossoming anew all the time all around us—now, in the spring, but not just now. The big beautiful stuff in the Bible isn't hard to see. You're familiar with it. You've noticed it before and probably appreciated its beauty. But there are also many small delicate, beautiful flowers, harder to find or even realize they exist, but stunning in their own way once you become aware they are there—individual verses and whole passages, waiting to be discovered where they've always been.

A lot of times you won't ever see them, unless somebody familiar with that sort of thing shows them to you. But once you've been shown, you can make them yours and enjoy the wonderful benefit yourself, and then share them with others who will also be blessed. That's why we study God's Word together. That's why Pastor Larry and I and others who've discovered hidden treasures over the years lead Bible studies. We're your "biblical yard guys." And that's why just coming to a group Bible study will give you quite a dazzling bouquet of scripture to show to others.

Yes, you can see the big, beautiful stuff without needing to have somebody point it out to you—stuff like the 23rd Psalm and some of the parables, the Christmas story and its colorful Old Testament cousins. But there's always more. There's always something so small and delicate that you've missed it and will continue to miss it until somebody points it out. That's why we say there's beauty and wonder in every bit of God's Word, and why we recommend you read it all, over and over again.

Every time you sit down to read God's Word—and especially when you sit down to discuss it with others—you are gathering divinely beautiful flowers that God has caused to bloom for you.

Every time you dig down deep into God's Word, you discover the never-before-seen blossom that God planted in your backyard ages and ages before you ever thought to look. And even the miniatures are marvelous. So, come pick some new biblical blossoms—we'll show you where to find them. And it's always peak season.

৵৵

60.

Going Places

Table. Tree. Tomb.

We have several important places to go over the next few days—several critical stops to make on this journey we're taking with God and each other through this world and this life. We're coming to the end of the challenging uphill climb we call Lent—walking the way of the penitent pilgrim. Like the journey Jesus took when He set His face toward Jerusalem, this season of spiritual examination and self-denying has offered us the opportunity to focus our minds and hearts more clearly on where we are going as His disciples, and what we will experience when we get there.

Our first stop is at a table, hidden away in an upper room. The table is set to commemorate the Passover, the meal for remembering and reenacting God's miraculous deliverance of His people—at great cost in life. And at the table, the memory of death passing over is transformed into the promise of life passing among and into all who come to the table in faith and submission. Tomorrow is Maundy Thursday, where, in the dim shadows of that room, the Lord *"prepared a table before [them] in the presence of [their] enemies;"* (Psalm 23:5). He prepares a table before us as well tomorrow night, where we may *"taste and see that the Lord is good;"* (Psalm 34:8, ESV).

The next stop is outdoors, in as starkly public a place as the previous one was private and withdrawn. As with the previous site, getting there will also require climbing. The destination is a tree—of sorts—on a hill. Stripped of its leaves and branches (save two), and of life itself, this tree's trunk sits in a hole, wholly without roots—torn from the earth, only to be returned—its only fruit, the abused and withering form of a remarkable Man—and more than a man. The tree is Calvary's Cross and we will stop there on Friday at noon to "see from His head, His hands, His feet, sorrow and love flow mingled down."[20] And if you choose to linger there to reflect and pray, your vigil will not go unrewarded.

The third stop—on Sunday morning—will bring us to a tomb—once new—now empty. The One Who served at the table and suffered on the tree, slept in the tomb. But He does so no longer. Once secured in death and sealed in darkness, He has broken the bonds of both, rising alive to realms of light…as you will see on this great Easter morning, if you heed the invitation extended to the first of His disciples who arrived here: *"Come, see the place where He lay…"* (Matthew 28:6, ESV). And the command that followed: *"Go quickly and tell…that He has risen from the dead…"* (Matthew 28:7, ESV).

We are approaching the most critical stops on our spiritual journey. I encourage you not to pass them by. If you stop at the table, it will touch your heart. If you stop at the tree, it will tear your heart like the veil in the Temple. If you stop at the tomb, it will take your heart and fill it with more joy and love and power than anything else in this world.

Lent is ending. The Passion and the Prize lie before us.

⤞⋅⤝

---

[20] From "When I Survey the Wondrous Cross," Isaac Watts, 1707.

61.

Another Anniversary

8 April

Tonight, Trinity celebrates its anniversary. Four years ago, we came together in the Village Hall, having given up so much, only to discover that God in His remarkable grace had given us so much more to replace what we had lost. And in the inexplicable euphoria of that evening, we agreed to be a church—or rather, realizing that we were a church already, we affirmed that fact to one another and agreed to proceed into the future together.

God, in His mercy, did not reveal to us at that time how hard the practical work would be to set up and sustain Trinity Christian Fellowship, and how many difficulties, disappointments and disagreements we would experience along the way. Instead, God showed us at the beginning how beautiful our fellowship would be and how real and strong and near His Holy Spirit would be. And we have overcome difficulties, endured the disappointments and refused to let disagreements disrupt the bonds of Christian love that have been, for many of us, like nothing we ever experienced in a church before.

And then there are those of you who are coming to, what is for you, a first or second or third anniversary celebration. You who have joined Trinity "along the way" are now a fourth to a third of our congregation. You are also the living proof that God has chosen to bless this church. Trinity is alive and strong because God continues to add to our fellowship individuals and families of faith who are finding what others found the first time we came together: God is doing something unusual and unusually good here, and the best thing you can do is be a part of it. And He has wanted you to share it and make it better and stronger by your presence and participation in our work and relationships. He is building the church He wants Trinity to be by drawing you here and grafting you into this living thing.

Tonight, we will nourish one another with our food and our fellowship. We will reflect on the past and imagine the future. And we will all recognize how fortunate we are to be a part of something so much bigger and more miraculous and more blessed than our individual parts in it. If you compare where we are now to where we were as each of the previous anniversaries arrived, you have to be impressed. If you could know what God is going to do with Trinity in the years to come, I suspect you would be even more impressed. A lot has happened to Trinity in its first four years, but God is just getting started.

Happy Anniversary, Trinity!

৯৽৾

62.

Blocking Out the Glare

29 April

You have probably noticed, if you have spent any time in our new facility, that the building is oriented so that the sun comes up on the Fellowship Hall side and goes down on the Music Room side. There are windows on all sides of the building, of course, but most of them are facing east and west—facing the sun in the morning or the afternoon. And on sunny days, that's an awful lot of light coming in through the windows. If you've been in the Fellowship Hall for a Sunday School class, or Fellowship, or a weekday meeting in the morning, you know what I'm talking about. Even with the sheers on the windows, the glare coming in from outside is so strong, you have a real problem seeing what's going on inside.

We'll get a permanent solution in place sooner or later, but one of the Sunday School classes got tired of not being able to see their lesson video on the TV screen and came up with a fairly effective temporary fix. The got a roll of black paper, which they cut into long strips, which they hung over the windows with clothes pins. By blocking out the glare from outside, they could see what they had been unable to see on the inside.

And there's a lesson for all of us. In this world where the glare from "outside" has become overwhelming all the time, it is almost

151

impossible to see with clarity what God would have us see on the "inside." And the glare is bad not just for a few hours in the morning or a little while in the afternoon; it literally never stops. The radio is always blaring. The TV is always broadcasting. The internet is always there with more material than anyone could ever absorb—and much of it bad. And for those involved in "social media," it's something every minute.

But what is the glare washing out that you want (and need) to see? The only way to find out is to block out the glare from outside. The folks in Sunday School came up with a "jury rigged" response and it worked quite well. In time, the response will become more effective still. But by not letting the outside influence in, they have been able to let the inside influence come out—to have its full and proper impact on them, by giving it a chance to come to them "clear and bright."

God sometimes helps the situation on Sunday mornings by providing a cloudy day to block the glare. In our lives, the "cloudy days" also seem to help us focus on the more important things "inside." But we also have to see the glare from outside for what it is and take our own steps to block it enough to see what God wants us to see inside. You will be amazed at what God is revealing when you can see it in His light.

❧

63.

The National Day of Prayer

6 May

Tomorrow is the National Day of Prayer. We have asked you to sign up to pray for a few minutes, sometime throughout the day, at church or at home. I encourage you to do so, whether you signed up or not.

The National Day of Prayer has become "institutionalized." It is scheduled every year about the same time, and there is a robust organization that promotes its observance by providing professional-quality promotional and supporting materials and by sponsoring elaborate, high-visibility events. This is not to be critical, but to recognize what must be done in our current culture to encourage people in our country to offer prayer for our country, even one day a year.

In times past, the political leader—a king or president—would merely issue a proclamation, directing or asking citizens to go to their local places of worship on a specified day to offer prayers of intercession in the face of a dire crisis, or prayers of thanksgiving in response to a great victory or deliverance from grave danger. And the citizens, by and large, would go and "do their duty." It was all part of a national consciousness that the foundation of any civilization is the religious component of its culture—the awareness that the affairs of individuals and whole societies are

153

continuously influenced (and ultimately determined) by God Himself. That national consciousness no longer exists in our country, which itself is sufficient cause for serious prayer on the part of those citizens who do still pray. The "prayerlessness" of our nation—and the faithlessness it reflects—are themselves the sign of a dire national crisis, given that the other part of the social reality—that God determines the fate of nations—has not changed. To believe that prayer is unnecessary, and even a waste of time, does not make it so, no matter how many people have come to that conviction.

And so, we pray with earnestness because so many others will not pray at all. And when the citizens of a nation (and its leaders) will not pray, they also will not listen to the God Who answers prayer—Who enters into a divine-human dialogue with those who do pray. If you will not listen, you cannot hear. But God will not ultimately allow Himself and His will to be ignored. God will break through the barrier of silence and speak to the "unpraying" a message that even deaf ears—and hardened hearts—cannot shut out.

And so we commit ourselves to praying tomorrow for our nation—and perhaps, more importantly, for those who have simply stopped praying, or now refuse to pray—because of the dire crisis the disappearance of prayer has brought upon our country. And though the institutionalized "National Day of Prayer" is but one designated day each year, the need of our nation for our intercessory prayers is not met in a single 24-hour period. We must pray for our nation every day, until our neighbors across the nation return to the practice of prayer—or until God tells us, as He told the Prophet Jeremiah, *"Do not pray for them anymore, for I will not listen—I will not hear..."* (Jeremiah 7:16; 11:14; 14:12, RSV).

Until then, as we say each Sunday in worship, "Let us pray..."

ॐ

64.

A Conversation about Music in Worship

10 June

Yesterday, I had the opportunity to spend some time, one on one, with our new Daybreak and NewSong pianist. Those of you who attended those services Sunday had the privilege of meeting him and the delight of hearing him play. Yesterday, he and I got together in the sanctuary to work out a couple of minor glitches in the process that presented themselves as we proceeded through his first Sunday at the keyboard. These were primarily things that I had not thought to tell him. (Reading the pastor's mind gets easier with practice; but it's not really fair to expect a musician to do it well right off the bat.)

We enjoyed a wonderful time of fellowship as we talked about how long to make the prelude and how fast to play the Doxology and when and how to serve him Communion. We worked out a number of adjustments in what and how and when he will play, and as the weeks go by, we will get our coordinated efforts close enough to perfection that you will think we're "there."

The other thing we talked about—okay, I talked, and he listened graciously—was the role of music in worship. I said, and he seemed to like the idea, that the music our musicians play and/or sing, in all of our services, is not done for our entertainment—or even our inspiration—because the reason for everything that worship leaders do is to give everyone attending the worship service the "equipment" for doing the work of offering God the worship that is everyone's responsibility.

Whatever the style or quality of the music—whatever the style or quality of the sermon—whatever the style or quality of any other part of the service—each person worshipping may make a judgment about, or have a personal response to, that style or quality. But if what instrumentalists, singers and sermonizers offer to God is pleasing to God, that's really what matters most. Will we sing our best and preach our best and pray our best and so forth? Yes, because any effort that is less than our best is not pleasing to God. And our best—regardless of how we (or others) measure it— is always pleasing to God.

The only inspiration that ultimately matters in worship is the inspiration that God chooses to bestow upon us as His gift. When we go to worship for our inspiration, we focus on ourselves and what we are getting out of the process. We do not focus on God as He has commanded us to do.

When we're *in* it for what we get *out* of it, the only thing we get out of it is what we (or others) put in it. God is left out of the process. And when the most you can possibly get out of it is what you or they put into it, you are more inclined to get very concerned about whether the music or the sermon or whatever else is "inspiring," because that's all you're going to get.

But if the sermon and the singing and the prayers and the scripture and the offering and communion and all the rest are actually your tools for helping you give God His rightful glory and thanksgiving, then every song you sing or hear is your opportunity to say, "Yes, Lord! That's my praise to You—that's what my heart is singing to You—every word of it!" And every sermon, no matter how short or long, weak or strong, is a stuttering attempt to say in human words what our holy God wants you to hear—to which you can respond, "Thank You, Lord, for revealing anything to me.

Speak Your divine message through this mortal messenger and say even more than his words can convey."

What happens to us as we worship is not the point of worship. The point is whether God gets from us what He wants. But when we worship God as He wants, what God does to us and for us, in the process, can (and likely will) be monumental—the truly inspiring grace and peace and power that God bestows on us when we focus every part of ourselves—heart, soul, mind and strength—on Him.

Our new pianist and I kind of see eye-to-eye on this, and we are both looking forward to bringing you—along with all our other worship leaders—the best of what God has equipped us to offer—so that you can offer God the best of what you have to offer—as your genuine work of worship.

ॐ

65.

Books

Like most pastors, I have a few books in my office. I have more in my study at home—and in the living room—and the den—and in our bedroom—and in the garage—and in bookcases and boxes in off-site storage. What can I say—I like books.

Most of my books are related to the Bible, or Christianity, or ministry, as you would expect. They're reference books. They tell me things I need to know or inspire me with their spiritual insight. Most of them, I've had forever. They're old friends—familiar faces smiling out at me from their designated spots on the shelves—or giving me the evil eye for not having spent more quality time with them recently.

A few of them, I spend a lot of time with—I read them over and over. Some, I just have to look at, and I'm reminded of some unforgettable bit of wisdom or truth they possess and have passed on to me. Some are relative strangers still, but I plan (or at least hope) to get to know them better later, when there's time. And some—not many—I realized right away I don't see eye-to-eye with at all, and I keep them around just to remind me of that and reconfirm my convictions. I wouldn't introduce them to any of my friends.

I have a shelf of Bibles. They're different colors and sizes. They speak with different "accents," all saying the same things in slightly different ways. On the shelf are all the Bibles I grew up with. The oldest and smallest still has pictures of Noah's Ark and David and Goliath and Jesus with the little children in it (with crayon scribbling on the back). The zipper it came with is long gone, though.

I can't gather all the people who have "spoken" to me across my life in my office or at home. And they wouldn't want to hang out in my storage unit. But a lot of wisdom, insight, encouragement and inspiration have come my way as a result of the people I have known, some briefly, some long and well. Some, I talk to frequently, even now. Some, I haven't heard from in years. Some, I will not see again on this side of the grave.

But like the books on my shelves, the people in my life are collected in my consciousness—still there to help form my perspective and firm up my resolve and find my way when I wander into unfamiliar territory.

Most of the people I've known in life have not written books. And most of the authors of the books I own I've never met personally. But I *have* met the Author of all my Bibles—personally. And no one has spoken more to me—in the pages of those Bibles, or in the course of my life—than Him. Yes, you get more out of a Bible by opening it and reading it than by letting it sit on a shelf. But you get far more still by meeting the One Who authored it. I'm always willing to introduce Him to my friends.

May the Author bless you.

৯৽৽৶

66.

Evil and Grace in a Charleston Church

24 June

Over the past week, we have seen and shared the horror of the mindless massacre of Christians in an historic Charleston church: American Christians, killed by an American, in America, as cruelly and callously as any Islamic terrorist in Africa or the Middle East.

The killer did not know the people he killed; they had done no harm to him or anyone else. He took their lives, not because of who they were, but because of *what* they were. Except that they weren't what he thought they were.

But that didn't matter to him—he had decided to kill simply to gratify a hatred he had decided to nurture in his heart. He went into a church, a house of God, where he, a stranger, was welcomed by these Christians and treated as a brother. He sat and listened as they studied the Bible and prayed—and then calmly took nine decent, distinguished lives. How dark this young man's heart! How dead his soul!

But when we are overwhelmed by darkness, we must look for light. And there is light here. It is not that the murderer has been caught and brought back to be tried for his atrocity. It is that those who loved the victims most—the survivors who suffer most as a result of this evil—have not returned evil for it. Though those gunned down cannot confront their killer, their loved ones can, and did, and in that first encounter, one after another said, "I forgive you."

This, too, made headlines, because it runs so counter to the way of the world. It's the way of Christ, Who forgave His own killers (Luke 23:34) and told His disciples to do the same to all who would do them harm (Luke 17:3-4). It's hard to believe that a person who has suffered such pain and loss at the hand of another could turn around the next day and say, "I forgive you," and mean it, as though saying it makes everything okay.

It doesn't, of course, and perhaps we should "unpack" what's really going on, so that we can see our way more clearly when we are called on to forgive those who hurt us—most of whom do so without such "malice aforethought." To say "I forgive you" in such a circumstance is not an end or conclusion, it is really only a beginning—but an essential, critical beginning.

The truth is that forgiveness really isn't an event—it's a process, whose length will be determined by the severity of the hurt one has experienced. To say the simple phrase, "I forgive you," does not erase all the natural emotions that well up and wash like waves over you in the aftermath of some significant suffering. But *deciding* to say the words—being able to say them—indicates a decision, or at least a desire, to *begin* the process of forgiving, which will take as long as it takes. It is the choice to turn toward light rather than slide deeper into darkness.

The grieving relatives will go a long time before their anger and pain, their sense of disbelief and emptiness, will subside to even manageable levels. These feelings will likely never go away entirely. But they have decided to mix in with them the mercy and grace and love that Jesus has given them, so that their negative thoughts and feelings will be made something else over time by the power of God.

They know that if they do not forgive—as the killer of their loved ones had not—they will become like him over time—

hardened in hatred. Forgiveness is a gift they are giving to this demonic young man—for their own sakes, as well as for his. If they do not embark on this long road of forgiveness, they will never get out of the dark place into which his evil has cast them. Their decision to be forgiving of his incredible crime is the sacred medicine that will heal them.

And it is, at the same time, an unmerited gift of grace—a lifeline of sacrificial love and hope offered to lift their deadly enemy out of the even darker place where he went on his own. Their forgiveness is a gift they know their Lord would have them give this dark soul of a man—because Jesus gave it to them when they needed it and could not get out of the darkness they had created for themselves.

I will think of them—and Him—the next time I bow in our church and say the familiar words: *"Forgive us our trespasses, as we forgive those who trespass against us,"* (Matthew 6:12, KJV).

∂∙∞

67.

Legal, But Not Right

Right and wrong—as opposed to legal and illegal—is determined for us by the God Who has redeemed our lives and reigns over us as Lord, not by public opinion or human authority. Morality is ultimately a matter, not of our personal preferences, but of God's revelation. And so, to give up our opposition to what God has said is wrong would require us to give up our faith and enter into rebellion against the One Who has directed us to be in opposition.

Let it also be said that we embrace a divinely directed code of morality even though none of us can meet its demands. We are not better people than our neighbors for our belief that the Bible is the ultimate source of authority about what is right. But no other position is open to us if we are to be obedient to God. We are faced with a *"not my will, but Thine, be done"* situation (Luke 22:42, KJV).

So let us be firm and resolute in our convictions, but also gracious, compassionate and humble. Let us forego insults and condescension in favor of reasoned explanations of the guidance provided us in scripture, and respectful engagement with those who do not agree with us, when the opportunity for conversation arises.

These are very emotional matters for many of us. But God would not have us make it our primary or exclusive focus. We still have the broad work of the church to do—in outreach, discipleship, worship and fellowship. Christians have always lived in a broken, fallen world, much of which, much of the time, has been openly opposed to God's will for us. In that, what happened last week[21] is just another reason God sent His Son to save us.

There are certainly difficult days ahead for Christians—and great days, too—if we give ourselves completely to our God Who has promised us peace that passes understanding and grace sufficient for all our needs.

る๛ら

---

[21] The U. S. Supreme Court's ruling legalizing homosexual "marriage" nationwide.

68.

Socks

Yesterday, I got up a little earlier than usual. I had some things I wanted to do before I headed to church. It was still fairly dark when I got up, especially with the blinds closed. But I got through the regular morning routine okay—until I got to the part about putting on my socks.

Now, my sock collection is, frankly, quite boring. I have nothing like the "dazzle" in my sock drawer that Ted and Bob and perhaps others enjoy. All my socks are a solid color, and though I do have more than one color in my collection, they are all dark and conservative: black, grey, brown and blue—navy blue (a color, by the way, never worn in the Navy).

Normally, a bunch of socks will go in the washer, come out of the dryer, be sorted and go neatly and logically into their color-coded sequence in the drawer. But they came out of the dryer a little late on Monday and were allowed to spend the night all mixed up together in a giant "sock slumber party" in the laundry basket. And there they all were the next morning, sleeping soundly, when I needed two of the designated color of the day (in this case, black).

In the shadows, I couldn't tell them apart, so I grabbed a handful and headed into the next room to examine them under a lamp. The browns were easy enough to eliminate—and the greys.

Finally, I had what looked like two black socks in hand and soon had them snuggled up over my foot and calf. All the rest went back into the basket.

I completed the process of dressing and went outside—out into the bright morning sun—to get the morning paper. And as I walked down the driveway, I glanced down to make sure my feet were alternating properly. That's when I noticed the black sock protruding below my left trouser leg—and then a blue one, beaming in its obvious blueness, rising up out of my right shoe. It wasn't even trying to look black.

Changing a sock after you're dressed is such a hassle—psychologically, if not physically—and for a moment, I debated with myself about just ignoring the discrepancy and living with it for a day. But then, I remembered I would be sitting in a circle with a dozen men in a few hours, and even they wouldn't buy the excuse that I was just trying to emulate Ted and Bob by adding a little "flash" to my "sock life."

So back I went to the laundry basket for another handful of dark socks. This time, I took them to the window and opened the blinds to let the sunlight in. In that light, I had no difficulty seeing the difference and knowing what was right.

So what did I learn?

The mistakes you make by trying to sort things out by a lesser light will be revealed for what they are in a greater light. Things that look the same in the shadows will not be able to conceal their fundamental differences when subject to true light. And sooner or later, everything will be brought out into the light.

Our world is growing increasingly content with making choices according to lesser lights. And as a result, we are seeing more and more mistakes and mismatches in what people think is right and how they "dress" their lives. The consequences are not pretty now, and they will only get worse, until the true Light is allowed to shine on the options everyone is considering each day. Let's let the true Light shine—on us—in us—and through us.

৵৽৵

69.

More Space

As I mentioned on Sunday, the office will be closing at noon on Friday for the holiday weekend. But even having the building open in the morning that day may be a challenge because we're supposed to have some folks working on the parking lot all day Friday and Saturday. I don't know exactly what they're going to do, but a part of the work will apparently involve repainting the lines that mark the parking spaces. And by repainting, I don't mean painting over where they are now, but painting them in different places—farther apart.

Someone said the spaces are eight feet apart now. Whatever the width actually is, most of us have discovered it's not enough. Pull in between two of the lines and you feel like you're threading a needle. And if there is a car in one or both of the adjacent spaces, it's easy to get a sense of sardine-ness. If you don't get in the space straight, and exactly in the middle (and who of us does all the time?), even getting in or out of your car can be an adventure in creative contortion.

The solution? Give ourselves more space. It's amazing what "a little more room" can do for your attitude and your ability to maneuver safely and comfortably in what had been a frustratingly confining environment. I'm looking forward to wider parking places. It will be better for me—and better for you if you're parking next to me.

Giving ourselves—and others—more "space" works much the same way for our relationships as it does for our parking. Sometimes we paint the "lines"—in the sense of our expectations and requirements—too close for comfort for ourselves, and too close for compliance for others. When we do, we tend to stress ourselves and judge others negatively.

But the core concept behind an interdenominational fellowship is painting the lines wider—giving everybody more room in our individual spaces because we know we are not going to get in our spaces perfectly straight or perfectly centered every time, or perhaps even any time.

We all "park our cars" differently. And whatever we think of each other's "parking," we're all doing the best we can. It's just easier for everybody if we widen all the spaces.

At the same time, we do need the lines. If we didn't have any, it would be chaos. You could park anywhere you wanted to, but one of two things would happen, and neither one would be good. You might end up with a whopping traffic jam, with people blocking other people in, or you would at least have people parking a lot farther away from each other than we need to, leaving less opportunity for people to get in the parking lot (and, therefore, less inclination to want to).

Clear lines, well-positioned, help us bring order and comfort to our process. They help us line up together, without crowding each other unnecessarily. Trinity has some clear lines—in what we believe, and in what we value—lines close enough to keep our faith strong and our fellowship connected, and wide enough to let us position ourselves with God individually without pressure to conform to someone else's way of "parking."

So, perhaps soon, pulling into Trinity's parking lot will be a more pleasant experience, as I hope finding your "space" in our Trinity fellowship already is.

இ௸

70.

Waiting for a Sign

It's not often I look out the window here and see a huge cement mixer driving through the parking lot. But that's what I saw yesterday. The rain had stopped (after many layers of "liquid blessings"), and workmen were out early near the north end of our property next to Highway 211, digging a big hole in the ground for the truck to dump cement in—to form a "footer," or foundation, for our new marque. First the cement, then the bricks, then the paint on the bricks, then the lettering, and then the secret will be out: "Trinity is here!"

We've waited a long time to put our name out there for the world to see. We were waiting, first of all, to get an overall design developed for the exterior renovation of the building so we would know how to make the sign "sync up" architecturally with what we are eventually going to look like on the outside. Then, of course, when we figured out what we wanted the sign to look like, what we figured out had to go to the Village "sign office" for approval, which we got last week. Then we got to wait a few more days on the weather.

And now, at long last, the work is underway. Thank you to everybody who had a hand in getting us there—and thank you to everybody who has waited patiently for something we all wanted

171

to see as soon as we got here. It gives that old phrase, "waiting for a sign," a whole new meaning.

We have waited for a lot of things over the course of our life together as Trinity. And it is true that some of the things we waited for and wanted most didn't happen at all. Yet so many dreams have come true, and are coming true, and will come true, by God's grace. And the disappointments have not deterred us from being the faithful fellowship God formed us to be.

How do we accomplish the things God wants us to do? We work together toward the common goal and vision, which we have done in many ways. But there is a line in the Healing Service liturgy that goes: "…we wait in faith and pray." And that, too, is an essential element in our life together, because we have learned over and over again that God is working with us according to His own agenda and timetable.

So now it seems that God is "giving us a sign." I expect when we see it finished and firm on its foundation, we will rejoice and be encouraged that, at last, the world at large will know who we are and "where we stand." And if this is a sign from God, what else are we to understand it to mean?

Perhaps that there is more to come in what God is doing with us, spiritually and physically. We know there are many other changes still in the works.

Some signs are like marques on the highway: you can't miss 'em. Others require us to wait patiently, and prayerfully, in firm faith, for the spiritual fog to lift, personally and corporately, so we can see what God is showing us.

And when the sign is there, firmly in place for all to see, the former frustrations will fade from our memories, because the joy of what now "is" will overwhelm the feelings we had of how hard it was to wait. I think that's a sign of how all things in our relationship with God will be.

క్రింది

71.

What to Wear

I woke up this morning thinking about "wearing the 'right' clothes for the occasion." That was always important in the military, as I learned to my embarrassment on those two or three occasions—over my 37-year-association with the Navy and Marine Corps—when I showed up for an event in the wrong uniform.

For many years, church families have struggled a bit about the business of what we ought to wear to worship, but that's a subject around which I do not expect the Christian community to reach consensus any time soon. And for that reason, I shall allow those unconscious canines to remain in their recumbent condition.

But we have several other events coming up in the next few days, before we worship together again on Sunday. Tonight, our monthly healing service will be held, and our dinner and study will follow, for which casual clothes have always been the uniform. (Yes, I wear a coat and tie, but that seemingly inexplicable sartorial aberration has not proven to be contagious, so "no worries" there.)

Tomorrow morning, many of us will meet for our annual church golf outing. The appropriate attire will feature comfort—and the fashion of the sport, no doubt. I have thought about bringing along one of those stylish carry bags you can buy in the grocery store to slide over my head and shoulders on those more than occasional occasions when my shots leave me too embarrassed to show my face to my friends. But since the goal is to keep the game moving as well as to win, perhaps my moments of mortification will be brief, even if frequently repeated.

Proper attire will also be important on Saturday, when we gather for a church-wide clean-up convention. Anyone who comes in a coat and tie, or an attractive wool skirt and sweater, will have their motives immediately and significantly suspected. Work clothes will be the uniform of the day, whether you find your appointed place of duty inside or out.

In the past, we have always tried to schedule these "property policing parties" on the hottest or coldest day of the year, but the forecast this time is for a partly cloudy day with 0 percent chance of rain, reaching a high of 72 degrees by the time we're done. (Our apologies to those who like to labor for the Lord under challenging meteorological conditions.)

Anyway, what we wear—and in the case of golf and grounds work—and the tools we bring to assist us—will have a lot to do with how well we perform and how happy we are when we're done for the day. And, as you have come to expect from me, there is a spiritual analogy: What we "wear" spiritually as Christians to all our earthly "events" is even more important, in the grandest scheme of things.

Paul provided a lot of spiritual fashion advice: *"...put on the Lord Jesus Christ...put on the new self...put on the whole armor of God...put on then, as God's chosen ones, holy and beloved, compassionate hearts, kindness, humility, meekness, and patience...and above all these, put on love, which binds everything together in perfect harmony..."* (Romans 13:14; Ephesians 4:24; 6:11; Colossians 3:12, 14, ESV). If the Bible is any indication, it seems that it is virtually impossible to be "spiritually" overdressed for any occasion. All of these items Paul mentioned will "go" with whatever you're planning to wear to dinner, to play golf, to clean up around the church and to worship

God within it. When we clothe ourselves in our proper spiritual attire, our Lord is likely saying, "I really love your outfit!"

୭~୭

72.

Another Halloween

Last week, I wrote about "wearing the right clothes for the occasion." I suppose I could stretch that subject for another week, given that millions of children, and more than a few adults, will be dressing up—or down—or, at least, differently—this Saturday.

Sundown Saturday brings on Halloween, a name derived from the fact that this day that begins at sundown and goes to sundown the next day (as ancient people measured days) is "All Soul's Day," which is also called "All Hallows." The names originally referred to all those folks who had died and actually made it to heaven. The long form of the term for that night was "All Hallows Evening," which was shortened in popular use to "Hallow-e'en."

As with most Christian holidays, there were competing pagan commemorations to contend with—in this case, "the spirits of the dead" who were not hallowed—holy—in heaven—or blessed or at peace—or anything positive like that. And so, while the Church was honoring those who had gone on to their eternal reward, the world around them focused on the idea of ghosts and evil spirits of the dead hanging around the earth—beings (or "non-beings") who weren't "happy campers" at all.

And, as usual, the worldly response was to use that idea as an opportunity to behave badly, kind of like the excesses of Mardi Gras the day before the beginning of Lent.

I bring this up to explain our reasoning for holding a Fall Festival on Halloween, as more and more churches are doing. There was a time in our history—a brief and closing window of time—when the redemptive influence of the Christian Church made it possible for communities to indulge in a little wholesome fun, with our children dressing up in costumes and collecting candy from the neighbors. It was great fun—and kept all the dentists in business.

But year by year, the world became a darker place and the wholesome was increasingly pushed aside for a harsher reality. An occasion for a little innocent fun has become something very different as people redefine the purpose of the day and indulge in ever greater excesses to satisfy their desire for unholy excitement.

And so, we do what the Church always does: we carve out an island of safety and sanity and godliness in a sea of turmoil and depravity. Saturday afternoon, we will set up shop on our little patch of holy ground, with trunks and hatchbacks open wide in welcome, to enjoy the simple pleasure of delighting our children, and others who take advantage of the opportunity we provide. We will taste the searing sauce of competing chilis and the sweetness of warm Christian fellowship. And we will be happy rather than haunted, whatever characters show up in their costumes. In this, as in everything we do, we will be celebrating what our Father in heaven has done for us—*"…hallowed be [His] Name"* (Matthew 6:9, KJV).

৯৵৹

177

73.

A Special Sunday

11 November

Well, it just goes to show: you really can't afford to miss a single Sunday at Trinity or you'll miss something wonderful. I've been fairly consistent in my attendance of late, but Joanne and I weren't in our usual seats this past Sunday, and something especially wonderful did happen: Trinity called its new Senior Pastor.[22] The vote of the members present was unanimous, 148 to 0. If Joanne and I had been there, we could have—and would have—made it an even 150 in favor. This is a tremendous blessing for Trinity.

I want to invite you to think with me for a moment about what happened Sunday at Trinity—from the divine perspective. We know what we were doing. Those of you who were present had your own personal experience of the process of listening to someone you may not have met before preach the Gospel of Jesus Christ, and then of being invited to extend to him your invitation to become your leader, instructor and companion in the spiritual journey you and all of us are sharing.

---

[22] I had announced to the congregation in early May that I had decided to retire from full-time pastoral ministry the following year (or earlier, if a suitable replacement could be found earlier). The church extended a call to my successor in November and I retired as Trinity's Senior Pastor in early January.

But beyond whatever happened on the human level, God was there, whether you knew it or not, just like He was there when Jacob woke up in the wilderness after dreaming about a ladder to heaven—woke up to the reality that God was in that place (Genesis 28:10-17). Our Pastoral Search Committee members have given testimony to God's presence in reflecting on their work to find God's choice for this position. Your new pastor saw God's hand at work on his side of things as God guided him through other ministry opportunities to us.

We called this man by having individual members make a simple mark on a single piece of paper. God has sent him to Trinity—given him to us as a gracious gift—by moving heaven and earth in miraculous and undiscerned ways (for who knows how many years) to mold him into what's "right" for us, and then making him *available* to us, and then *known* to us, and, finally, so *impressive* to us that we, with our many different perspectives, would all vote to endorse what God has already done for us.

The pastor of a church is always and only—at best—an instrument in the hand of God, through which God works in the lives of a group of people who have agreed to be a community of faith, following Jesus Christ. Whatever you think of the instrument itself—whatever "qualities" it might have, in and of itself—it is the Hand that holds it and wields it to accomplish a higher and holy intention that gives the instrument its true value. Pastors and people alike do well to remember that pastors are servants of God first, and only then servants of a church and its people. And if not the first, useless and perhaps dangerous as the second.

It is good and fitting, I think, that this process comes as we approach the season of Thanksgiving, for the proper response to his being called unanimously—and his enthusiastic acceptance of that call—is gratitude to God. We have much to be thankful for this year.

74.

The Paris Attacks

18 November

We have been awash this week in the news coverage of the multiple massacres in Paris. You cannot look at your television or newspaper (or computer or cellphone) without seeing scenes of stunned and grieving survivors building memorial mounds at the places of carnage—shrines of flowers, candles, cards—and tears. And around the world, iconic buildings have been bathed in sympathy and solidarity—covered in the national colors of the country where monsters disguised as men worshipped their false god of death by taking the lives of as many people as possible who did not deserve to die.

We are told that it was a failure of intelligence—that the murderers have gotten wiser in the ways of avoiding detection as they prepare to unleash hell on a peaceful and unprepared public. But technology is not the trouble when human beings sink below the level of animals. It just amplifies the problem.

The truth is that there is no limit to the depravity a sinful mankind is capable of when we reject the God Who created us. Those who reject the one true God always chose another—whether themselves or a defective rival—to worship, to serve and obey. Some other value system, moral code, and way of life will take the place of the one God calls all people to embrace.

We have seen the worst—we hope—in Paris, as we did in our own country on 9/11. But our appropriate distress in recent days over the lesser-but-no-less-real depravity in our own culture and society is fruit of this same rejection of God's authority. And we ourselves are not immune from the temptation to evil within our own hearts, which is why we must be diligent in our attention to the Holy Spirit, Who is always leading us toward His holy light and away from demonic darkness. And if there is worse to come, we will need all the strength, courage and hope our faith can afford us.

In the meantime, I think it is a good thing to show our sympathy for so many who have suffered so much, and our solidarity with those who are seeking to attack evil at its source. It turns out, in this case at least, that "their colors" are also "our colors." Civilization is better than savagery, and we support the best of humanity in this broken world of ours by living our commitment to Christ—and showing His "colors" to the world around us as well.

ॐ

75.

It's a Miracle

25 November

A major, near-miraculous milestone in the life of our church occurred recently with virtually no fanfare, and I think that oversight should be corrected. Last week (or perhaps the week before—even I'm not sure), we finally emptied out the off-site storage unit Trinity first rented a year and a half ago when we began preparing our move from our rented spaces to our present property.

You may not remember the chaotic conditions we encountered as we worked to make room for the Sandhills Classical Christian School's Pre-school to take over and remodel our old spaces on Route 5 weeks before we were able to begin bringing our own stuff here. We had to get a lot of that stuff out of those spaces quickly. And even after we relocated here, we couldn't bring a lot of the material things we had amassed in our first three years together with us right away—because we were going to spend the first four and a half months tearing up the interior to achieve the improvements we now enjoy. So the only solution was off-site storage.

Why is this recent milestone so worthy of commemoration (besides the monthly rent we will no longer be paying)? I think it has to do with Newton's Fourth Law of Motion that I seem to remember learning in school. This is the proven scientific law that "objects placed in temporary storage tend to remain in temporary storage permanently."

So how were we able to break this fundamental law of (human) nature? Well, we finally focused our attention on what we actually had left in the garage-sized room down the road—and decided to "do something" with everything there. Some things—things we had not needed in 18 months and couldn't see a need for in our new circumstances—were sold or donated to charities. The rest— mainly boxed-up church library books—were laboriously loaded on a personal pick-up truck and brought here, where they have been stored neatly and safely in the small storage shed in the tree line.

Soon, the most useful of these books will line up side by side on the shelves of several bookcases we have obtained and placed in the far corner of the Music Room to serve as our budding library. And, when it is emptied out, the small shed outside will be replaced by a newer and larger one—because, as we all know, the only "givens" in life are "death and taxes"[23]—and the need for more storage.

 howgee

---

[23] Benjamin Franklin referred to the "certainty of death and taxes" in a letter he wrote in 1789 about the chances of success for the U.S. Constitution. However, other authors in the early part of that century had also quoted the phrase. My favorite reference to it is from what is probably an apocryphal story about an elderly European monarch taking her last breaths. Her royal chaplain tried to comfort her by reminding her piously that there was nothing certain in life but death. To which she responded faintly but firmly—"…and taxes."

76.

Christmas Decorating

2 December

Saturday morning, a small multitude of our members came to church to decorate it for Christmas. It was our first time to do this; last year in December, we were deep into the inside renovations, and still holding our worship services at O'Neal (see footnote, page 34). But this year, as the outside of the building comes apart in preparation for its new look, our cast of colorful characters gathered in the spiritual and physical warmth within these walls to deck the halls with symbols of the Savior's coming.

Some of us had some ideas of how the deed should be done—we had been thinking about "things decorative" for weeks. Most showed up simply to do whatever they were assigned (or their hands "foundeth") to do (see Ecclesiastes 9:10, KJV). What we found as we began to get organized and see who we had and what they would have to work with, was that some things went naturally according to plan, and some things required some additional planning on the spot.

For instance, when asked about Christmas music as background for our work, we realized we hadn't thought of that at all. But since inexperienced experimentation with the sanctuary sound system seemed ill-advised, a diligent search of the closets in the children's classrooms turned up a portable CD player, and one or two folks who didn't live too far away made quick trips home to retrieve their favorite Christmas recordings, and the decorating soon developed an appropriately themed soundtrack.

కాంత

Some of us brought brute force to bear on things like lifting trees up on to raised platforms and moving ladders (necessary, but dangerous items) around the rooms. Some devoted themselves to the delicate details of whipping up wreaths and building bows and gathering garland to give doors and sconces a festive feel. We found enough lights to brighten even more than the three Christmas trees that had been donated to the cause.

At one point, we did cause a scene—a nativity scene. You can see it from either side of the westernmost window in the foyer. And, yes, the manger is missing its Baby Jesus, but that's only because we're still in Advent, the season when we await His coming. Rest assured, our Lord will arrive where He is supposed to be on Christmas Eve.

We had a great time together Saturday morning, and were delighted with the results of our labor alongside each other. We also now have a starting point for figuring out what to do differently or better next year—and what to do exactly the same because some of what we did—if not all of what we did—was absolutely wonderful.

But here's something else to think about: while the goal of all the hours of work on Saturday was to do something dazzlingly beautiful for all to see, its greater purpose was to glorify God. And though most of what we come together to do—what we devote countless hours and effort to accomplish here—is not undertaken to dazzle anyone, virtually everything we do here at Trinity is beautiful in a spiritual sense. Every ministry we engage in has the same greater purpose as the decorating done last week—to glorify God. And God—Who sees the good we intend in all we do—is delighted by the sight of all our "decorating"—even if we only decorate our own hearts with our otherwise unseen efforts to seek Him and serve Him and please Him.

怘•怙

77.

Christmas Singing

9 December

Tonight, we sing! Despite our after-dinner full stomachs and whatever deficiencies we may have—individually and collectively—in the making of music, we will unite our voices in celebration of our coming Christ, and warm our hearts with the familiar words of carols we have known and loved since childhood. No person or group will "perform" for us, we will simply sing the story of Christmas ourselves—and our praises to God for it.

Why are we going to spend the evening singing? Because people want to. We were asked to devote this last Wednesday evening we will spend together before Christmas to singing these wonderful, well-known songs.

But it goes deeper than that. Last week, I mentioned that, early in the decorating process at church, someone asked, "Where's the Christmas music?" It wasn't that the dialogue had died down—that we couldn't think of anything to say to each other. There was just a natural sense that a particular kind of music was appropriate and desirable to accompany what we were doing. I had not thought about it ahead of time or made arrangements for music to be available, but people recognized right away that something was missing. And we scurried to fill the gap—even in a make-shift way.

But consider that we bring music to every important process in our lives, if we can. We worship with music, of course. It is often the most powerful part of the process. We bring a particular kind of music to funerals and weddings. We sing or play patriotic music on civic holidays and at times of national crisis or accomplishment. With music, we are able to experience and express the emotional, psychological, and even spiritual significance of our circumstances more clearly and deeply than our logical, intellectual processes will generally allow. As with movies, our lives seem to make more sense with an appropriate and moving "soundtrack" supplied.

But it may go farther and deeper even than that. For centuries, poets, scientists and philosophers have talked of something they call "the music of the spheres"—a spectacular harmony in all of Creation, large and small—the dependable and discernable rhythm of the stars and planet in their orbits—the order and precision of so much of our world, whether living or inert. [24] The psalmists and the prophets were inspired to call forth songs of praise and rejoicing from the heavens and the earth, as well as from all mankind. When Jesus was told to stop His disciples from singing His praises, He replied, *"...if these were silent, the very stones would cry out,"* (Luke 19:40, ESV).

Music, it seems, is a significant way God communicates with us. And music is, therefore, an important way we are able to communicate with God. So tonight, we satisfy our sense of wanting to sing familiar carols. And in the process, perhaps, we say something important to God that we would find it very difficult to say as well in any other way. Perhaps we will be saying something to God in our singing that God dearly desires to hear from us. I wonder what He will say to us.

৵৽৽ও

---

[24] See also "This Is My Father's World," Maltbie D. Babcock (text) and Franklin L. Sheppard (tune, adapted from a traditional English melody), 1915.

78.

Of the Father's Love Begotten

23 December

Tomorrow at five o'clock, those in town and able will gather for a Christmas Eve service to hear the familiar story from the Bible and sing familiar carols about that story. It will be a service with a celebratory and probably somewhat chaotic "feel," with kids squirming in excited anticipation as the last hours to Christmas count down.

Friday morning, a smaller and calmer group will gather to worship with the reverent words of a moving liturgy written long ago—and some of the same songs we will have sung the night before sung again, with and for "comfort and joy." Both services will be beautiful in their own way because the focus of both services—the only reason for holding them—is the most beautiful thing in all the world and all of human history: the birth of our Messiah.

Many songs have been written about our Messiah and His birth—some familiar, some not. Some of the least familiar are also some of the most beautiful. I'm going to "cheat" a little with my letter this week because I want to offer, as a Christmas gift of sorts, the words of one of those beautiful songs you may not hear this Christmas—and may not even know. A wonderful musician who worked with me in several Navy chapels years ago first shared it with me, and it has been very special to me ever since.

The English words are translations of an ancient Latin poem. The haunting melody (which I can't reproduce here, of course) originated as a medieval "chant," the kind you can imagine echoing upward in majestic cathedrals. The carol is entitled, "Of the Father's Love Begotten."[25]

> Of the Father's love begotten,
> Ere the worlds began to be,
> He is Alpha and Omega,
> He the Source, the Ending He,
> Of the things that are, that have been,
> And that future years shall see,
> Evermore and evermore!
>
> He is found in human fashion,
> Death and sorrow here to know,
> That the race of Adam's children
> Doomed by law to endless woe,
> May not henceforth die and perish
> In the dreadful gulf below,
> Evermore and evermore!
>
> O that birth forever blessèd,
> When the virgin, full of grace,
> By the Holy Ghost conceiving,
> Bore the Saviour of our race;
> And the Babe, the world's Redeemer,
> First revealed His sacred face,
> Evermore and evermore!

---

[25] "Of the Father's Love Begotten," from a medieval chant, English words by John Mason Neale and Henry Baker, 1861.

This is He Whom seers in old time
Chanted of with one accord;
Whom the voices of the prophets
Promised in their faithful word;
Now He shines, the long Expected,
Let Creation praise its Lord,
Evermore and evermore!

Righteous Judge of souls departed,
Righteous King of those alive,
On the Father's throne exalted
None in might with Thee may strive;
Who at last in vengeance coming
Sinners from Thy face shalt drive,
Evermore and evermore!

Christ, to Thee with God the Father,
And, O Holy Ghost, to Thee,
Hymn and chant with high thanksgiving,
And unwearied praises be:
Honour, glory, and dominion,
And eternal victory,
Evermore and evermore!

We can thank John Mason Neale and Henry Baker for the beautiful English words. But as the words suggest, for the all-surpassing beauty of the Subject of the words—the Gift of God born to us in human form—we must thank our heavenly Father alone.

৵৽৾

79.

Coming to the End

30 December

The last few days of another year are fast fading into history. It is an odd time. The warmth and beauty of a Christmas barely past linger still, while the impulse of energy that a new year automatically awakens within has not yet arrived. My natural tendency is to become nostalgic, to ponder the deeper meaning of things that have happened—both public and private—and to bring to mind people who were, and remain, important to me. These are days that seem to invite reflection and encourage us all to put what we have experienced in some productive place in our perspective about the grander scheme of our lives and God's plan.

Most of us have endured our share of disappointments this year. Some of us have survived, if only barely, the greatest of sorrows. We have all been surprised by the unexpected, whether good or bad. We have made mistakes and observed the mistakes of others, and found that we could "get past" both. We have worried terribly about any number of things, only to see them work out somehow. And there have been wonderful moments of joy— always fewer than we would have liked, of course—but enough to bring a smile and sense of appreciation even in the act of remembering.

Yes, some things are coming to an end—as they always do in this life—and the awareness of that part of life's process is heightened at this time of year. But new and wonderful things are also beginning, and a new year encourages us to look beyond our nostalgia to the good gifts our great God is waiting and planning to give us—the God Who has promised to *"make all things new,"* (Revelation 21:7, RSV).

May God give us the grace to make peace with the past so that we can look forward with hope and courage to the future.

৵৽

80.

Last Word

6 January

Today is Epiphany, the day each year when the Church has commemorated the arrival of the Wise Men to see and worship the newborn King of the Jews. "Epiphany" is a Greek word that means "appearance." Matthew (2:1-11) tells us that the Wise Men appeared at the house where Jesus and His family were, in Bethlehem. But it is the appearing of Jesus—God Incarnate—and especially His appearing to the Gentiles (represented by the non-Jewish Wise Men who were drawn to Him by a divinely-appointed star)—that we celebrate.

Our Lord has appeared many times to many of us in these past few years that we have spent together. We have had many "Epiphanies" to inspire and bless us on our shared spiritual journey.

Last Sunday was one of those days for me. You honored me far beyond what most people are ever privileged to experience.[26] I am—and will always remain—extremely humbled and tremendously grateful for your love, kindness and affirmation. I could say more, but I could never say enough. I can never say thank

---

[26] The Pastor Emeritus offered an *encomium* (a term I had never heard before) to my ministry as his sermon and the congregation held a "testimonial" luncheon for me after church in a lovely banquet hall nearby.

you enough—or to enough people—for last Sunday—or for all the help I have received in serving as your pastor over these years. But I want to say a little about the latter.

I want to thank every one of you who trusted me to lead you and love you, and affirmed me in my efforts, whether effective or not. I want to thank so many of you who shouldered the weight of leadership in the many ministries we have undertaken together. I want to thank those of you who took the thankless—and often unseen—tasks in hand and worked long and hard for the good of this church. I want to thank those of you who forgave me when I offended you or frustrated you with what I did or didn't do. I want to thank all of you who have worked alongside me to help build and sustain Trinity in this remarkable spiritual adventure God called us to undertake together.

ॐॐ

And, finally, the most important thank you is reserved for the ministry partner who would prefer I not say even this much. Joanne has been my "personal pastoral pit crew" every day that I have been with you. Keeping as low a profile as she could get away with, she has recharged my batteries, assessed the damage incurred in the course of "the race" and expertly repaired it, offered insight for more effective performance that always turned out to be inspired, whether I properly respected and applied it or not.

She celebrated my successes and suffered my setbacks with me and sent me back out every day when she would rather have sheltered me from the struggles that awaited as we worked to build and strengthen Trinity. She has blessed you far more than you can know.

She and I love you, and will remember you—and what God has blessed us all to share together.

God be with you till we meet again.

ॐॐ

Indices

Letters in Alphabetical Order

Letters in Alphabetical Order

Letters in Alphabetical Order

Letters in Alphabetical Order

Letters in Alphabetical Order

www.ingramcontent.com/pod-product-compliance
Lightning Source LLC
Chambersburg PA
CBHW020852090426
42736CB00008B/345